When I minister with R es
around America, I'm alway us
downloads he gets—and th he
releases what the Lord speaks to his heart. In *Supernatural Access*, Ryan takes you on a journey with the Holy Spirit into the prophetic realm. With inspiring insight and practical instruction in every chapter, you'll soon learn how to gain supernatural access you've been praying for. Whether you are new to the gifts of the Spirit or are seasoned in prophetic release, this book will open your eyes to a new level of the supernatural.

—JENNIFER LECLAIRE
SENIOR EDITOR, *CHARISMA*
SENIOR LEADER, AWAKENING HOUSE OF PRAYER

God hasn't stopped talking, but we have lost the art of listening. Hearing the voice of the Lord is critical to a life of intimacy with Him, to a walk of faith, and to success in life. Ryan LeStrange does a masterful job of reintroducing us to this life-changing wonder: hearing the voice of Father God.

—DUTCH SHEETS
INTERNATIONALLY KNOWN CONFERENCE SPEAKER
AUTHOR, *INTERCESSORY PRAYER*

Ryan LeStrange is one of the most prolific apostolic and prophetic voices in our day. This dynamic book will radically transform your life with great insight, revelation, and impartation. It's a *must* read.

—BRIAN GUERIN
FOUNDER OF BRIDAL GLORY INTERNATIONAL

People tell me all the time, "I don't hear God's voice." The tragedy is that God is always speaking, but very few people know how to discern the data. Ryan LeStrange has written a must-read book for anyone eager to learn the numerous ways God communicates with His children. Get ready to engage with the practical activations embedded within each chapter that are uniquely designed to help boost your confidence in supernaturally accessing the heart of God.

—DARREN STOTT
LEAD PASTOR, SEATTLE REVIVAL CENTER

In this powerful book, apostolic forerunner and prophetic voice Ryan LeStrange gives the believer a spiritual road map into hearing, understanding, and responding to the voice of God. You will not only receive deep insight into the supernatural, but you will also be activated in the supernatural skills, discerning the heartbeat of God for every area of life. As you read this essential manual, I believe you will be equipped to hear God's voice on a level you have yet to experience.

—KYNAN T. BRIDGES
AUTHOR OF *90 DAYS OF POWER PRAYER*
AND *UNMASKING THE ACCUSER*
SENIOR PASTOR OF GRACE & PEACE GLOBAL FELLOWSHIP

I want to highly recommend this amazing new book, *Supernatural Access*, by my friend Ryan LeStrange. This book is a guide into the supernatural that will give you access into heavenly gates, windows, doors, and realms by the Holy Spirit and will impart revelation knowledge to all who read it. God is supernatural, and we are called to live the supernatural life. There is a twenty-first century new breed prophetic company emerging in this generation that will rise up above the normative mind-set of the day. This Daniel company will display incredible new miracles, healings, signs, and wonders and break open revival in churches, cities, regions, and nations across the globe. If you are part of this new breed company and one of the hungry ones, then this book will serve as a preparatory guide to living a life of the miraculous for you.

—JEFF JANSEN
SENIOR LEADER, GLOBAL FIRE CHURCH, GLOBAL CONNECT, GLOBAL FIRE MINISTRIES INTERNATIONAL
AUTHOR OF *GLORY RISING*
AND *THE FURIOUS SOUND OF GLORY*

Ryan LeStrange has delivered another great book that is so needed on the imperative subject of revelatory release. I've always felt that so many people in the body have never been given tools and much-needed principles on tuning into God's voice. It's common knowledge that we can't become His voice to our world until we first hear His voice. Revelation is the combination code to an entire realm where impossibilities become realities. I believe that a next-level signs and wonders movement is about to hit the earth, and it will trigger an unprecedented harvest. In your hand is a manual to launch into this dynamic. This book should be read by all who want to be used by God for the more He has ordained for this hour.

—SEAN SMITH
AUTHOR OF *I AM YOUR SIGN* AND *PROPHETIC EVANGELISM*

Supernatural
ACCESS

RYAN LeSTRANGE

CHARISMA
HOUSE

Most CHARISMA HOUSE BOOK GROUP products are available at special quantity discounts for bulk purchase for sales promotions, premiums, fund-raising, and educational needs. For details, write Charisma House Book Group, 600 Rinehart Road, Lake Mary, Florida 32746, or telephone (407) 333-0600.

SUPERNATURAL ACCESS by Ryan LeStrange
Published by Charisma House
Charisma Media/Charisma House Book Group
600 Rinehart Road
Lake Mary, Florida 32746
www.charismahouse.com

Cover design by Lisa Rae McClure
Design Director: Justin Evans

Visit the author's website at www.RyanLeStrange.com.

Library of Congress Cataloging-in-Publication Data:
Names: LeStrange, Ryan, author.
Title: Supernatural access / Ryan LeStrange.
Description: Lake Mary, Florida : Charisma House, 2017. |
Includes
   bibliographical references.
Identifiers: LCCN 2017029173| ISBN 9781629991689 (trade
paper) | ISBN
   9781629991696 (ebook)
Subjects: LCSH: Listening--Religious aspects--Christianity. |
God
   (Christianity)--Will. | Revelation. | Supernatural.
Classification: LCC BV4647.L56 L47 2017 | DDC 234/.13--dc23
LC record available at https://lccn.loc.gov/2017029173

17 18 19 20 21 — 987654321
Printed in the United States of America

I dedicate this book to all the lovers, dreamers, creatives, prophets, and prophetic people out there. I dedicate this to the brave, the daring—those who are bold enough to seize the moment, unlock the promise, and go for it in the realm of the Spirit! There is an amazing company of kingdom people arising who passionately love Jesus in all of His glory and want to know and be known by Him. They are tired of living without the compass of Holy Spirit tuned in and active. They want to hear His voice clearly and do exploits. They have been born for more.

CONTENTS

ACKNOWLEDGMENTS

THANK YOU TO my amazing wife, Joy—the love of my life! Thanks to my son, Joshua, and my mom, Eileen; both help me in so many ways. Thanks to the staff, team, friends, and partners who stand with me and help me fulfill the mandate upon my life.

Thanks to all of my wild prophetic friends who challenge me, teach me, and urge me to go deeper. I am not satisfied; I am thankful, but there is still a more in my heart! Thanks for helping me in my journey into the more.

Thank you to the fathers and mothers in various streams and movements. Thank you to the forerunners! I acknowledge you—I salute you, and I thank God for you. Your obedience has helped unlock the destiny of a generation.

Thanks to my publisher and the amazing team there who help turn messages into manuscripts and work diligently to get the word out.

FOREWORD

I LOVE THE TITLE to this book: *Supernatural Access*. I wish I had thought of it first! Mercy—it is perfect! I love the subtitle to this book: *Remove Roadblocks in Order to Hear God and Receive Revelation*. I wish I had come up with that! It is brilliant! I love the accessible approach of this book. I love the tone of this book. I love the scriptural content of this book.

Do you want me to keep going on? I can...Follow my train of thought for a little bit longer.

Ryan LeStrange openly states that he talks too loud, gets impetuous, and is madly in love with his wife! Oh my goodness. Sounds like me a few years ago. I mean that! (OK, some say I still talk too much and too loud. I know...) But as I opened the pages to this descriptive manuscript, I saw my own life's prophetic journey and pilgrimage everywhere. That is so rare. Wow! I am excited!

Why am I so excited? Do you know how many forewords and endorsements I have written for people? (I actually do not have a clue, and if you know the answer to that off-the-cuff statement, then you are definitely a prophetic trivia nut.) Moving on.

Yes, I am excited. I just found a next-generation, passionate prophetic personality wired a lot like me. Ryan

LeStrange (Le…what?) embodies his message. He and his word are one. He does not just move in the gifts of the Holy Spirit; he is a gift. He does not just teach on hearing God; he activates others into the realms he walks in. Mercy! I like this guy.

More important than my exuberant display of excitement is the concrete content contained in this sound prophetic writing. The house you build will only be as strong as the foundation you pour. Jesus said that before you build a tower, you are to sit down and count the cost.

I understand these type of statements a whole lot better today than I did thirty years ago. Every house is going to have wind and waves come against it, but the house that is built upon the solid rock of Jesus and His words will stand. Why am I mentioning this?

This is not a fluffy, hyperprophetic book. This is a well-grounded and biblically sound set of teachings that comes from a life laid down for God. Thank you, Ryan, for being faithful to your calling. Thank you for offering this generation a look at what a true supernatural lifestyle can look like.

One thing is lacking though—there should be a warning label on the cover of this book. It should say something like this: "Warning! If you want to continue living a boring Christian life, don't read this book!"

Abundantly pleased!

—Dr. James W. Goll
Founder of God Encounters Ministries
International Speaker
and Best-Selling Author

INTRODUCTION

GUESS I HAVE always been a radical. I have never been a half volume, half-hearted kind of guy. I go in strong, and I go in full force. I can relate to Peter. I too sometimes jump before I have properly measured the distance, and I sometimes speak before I have thought the whole thing through. I am a passionate person who loves a sense of adventure. I have lost count of the times that my wife has told me that I am being too loud. I tend to forget about other people when I am excited and relaying a story! This does not always work out well in a public place.

It is with this personality that I came into the gospel. I was drawn to the supernatural as a child but did not have a grid for it. I was not raised in a home that taught me the gospel message because much of my family simply did not know it. I explored the realm of spirits, looking for answers. The enemy sent dark influences into my life, opening me up to the demonic realms. Then my salvation experience came, and I was radically set ablaze by the power of God. My life took a bold turn toward the call of God, and I found myself leaving everything that was familiar to step out into the unknown.

Over the next twenty years I experienced countless miracles, breathtaking prophetic encounters, and a life of the supernatural. Today I am hungry for more. I don't read the Bible as a nice little book of principles and suggestions but as a daring call to explore the farthest reaches of an unending God and His supernatural kingdom.

I read the exploits of Paul, turning the known world upside down, and my spirit leaps! I love to explore the deliverance call of Moses, with signs and wonders abounding. One thing stands out to me: God is by nature supernatural! There is no place in the Word of God for "normal living" trapped in this earthly realm. We are born-again children of God endued with supernatural power.

We seem to be trapped in a religious haze. Much of the Western church holds God as an idea that they fit somewhere into their busy lives. He is a part of their lives, but they only go to Him when trouble strikes or they need a blessing. He is a concept, an idea, or a theology but not an actual person from another realm who has become their fascination and the central theme of their whole lives. Pastors spend countless hours trying to plan events and programs to entertain a bored and weary church. Why are they so bored? Why are they in such a rush to get in and out of a gathering? Could it be because they are empty and thirsty due to the void of authentic, New Testament ministry? When was the last time that we saw a megachurch pastor in the Western world stop a well-planned service because God's presence filled the building and began to heal people? Why don't we see this more? After all, this was the primary operation of the early church. Why are churches, ministries, and revival hubs that boldly pray for the sick, prophesy, and cast out devils considered weird by Western Christians? What is weird is that people claim to believe in Jesus and follow the teachings of Paul without any of the signs following! The early church was not built on well-organized religious programs but on radical revival and supernatural encounters. It is weird to be a Bible believer and not heal the sick! It is weird to be filled with the Spirit and not function in the gifts.

> My speech and my preaching was not with enticing words of man's wisdom, but in demonstration of the Spirit and of power, so that your faith should not stand in the wisdom of men, but in the power of God.
> —1 CORINTHIANS 2:4–5

The reality is this: God is a supernatural God! When we were born again, we became spiritual beings alive to God and living in an earthly realm. We are supernatural people called to manifest the kingdom of God. The supernatural should be completely normal to us. Read the Bible. Moses parted the Red Sea. Elijah called fire from heaven. Elisha raised a woman's son from the dead. Jesus walked on water, raised a dead man, cast out a legion, and then rose from the dead. Paul and the apostles rocked the known world with many signs and wonders. They subdued demon rulers, shook territories, and impacted a generation. Today's Western church world looks nothing like the early church. The Bible is not a book about boring people in predictable gatherings exercising well-thought-out plans. It is a book filled with spontaneous and powerful supernatural wonders.

This book is a manifesto for supernatural living, God encounters, and radical prophetic leading. You are standing at the doorway into the dimensions of the Spirit. I want to lead you down the pathway of exploration into the kingdom and all of its glory. Mundane living is not your portion, and watered-down revelation is not your inheritance. You can be effectively led by Holy Spirit. You can know and discern the will of God for your life. You can operate in tremendous miracles and authority. You can receive and walk in more. The supernatural life is for you.

As you read the words on these pages, my prayer is that something deep within you springs to life. God is breathing on the hidden dreams and desires of your heart. The lies of the enemy are being chipped away and the confidence of a son or daughter is arising. You are a child of God, born into His kingdom with all the rights and privileges of an heir. Let's journey deep into the mystery and wonder of our majestic Father.

CHAPTER 1

CREATED TO HEAR FROM GOD

· · · · · · · · · · · · · · · · ·

One Word Redirects My Life

A T SIXTEEN YEARS old I had a radical encounter with God that forever shifted my life. I had come to a painful low in my life. I know that you are probably thinking that I was just a kid, so what did I have to be depressed about? I would think exactly the same thing. The reality is that I had been under heavy assault from the enemy since early on in my life. At sixteen I knew what it was like to sink deep into the pit of depression and hopelessness. In the middle of this struggle the love of Jesus reached me. Not only was my heart turned away from sin and bondage, but also I was set ablaze with Holy Spirit fire.

The assault I experienced began when I was young. I encountered a spirit of fear as a child when a relative locked me in a closet and told me spooky stories. My thirst for fear grew as I began to watch every horror movie that I could. It is amazing how deception works! In my confused state I actually craved the very thing that was feeding my bondage. It was a trap the enemy laid out for me. Fear was so alive in me and the sense of fear so vivid in my life that I could smell it, sense it, and taste it.

This was not my only struggle. Growing up without a firm understanding of who God is and His plan for me left a vacuum in my life. That void was filled with many wrong voices and decisions. The more I explored ungodly avenues for the supernatural, the more I encountered darkness. It was like a web that continued to ensnare me, and I was deceived into being a willing participant.

By the time that I found Jesus, I was confused, oppressed, and hurting. Shortly after my experience of Jesus's love reaching me, I began to listen to teaching from various ministers. One in particular would preach about faith and miracles; I had never heard such authority. Most of the preachers whom I encountered in my beginning days with God were charismatic, well-spoken, and confident, but they were not confrontational, radical, or bold. As I listened to stories about unwavering faith and tremendous miracles, something inside me began to leap! I could feel a stirring deep down in the midst of my being. At the time I had absolutely no idea what I was sensing.

I kept listening, kept praying, and kept learning as the divine prompting continued. The more I listened to this particular teacher, the more my inner man was stirred. One day I heard him mention that he had a Bible college. I just knew that I needed to go! Those moments are difficult to explain; I have had many encounters with God when He has vividly spoken to me through dreams, visions, and other supernatural occurrences, but this was just a knowing and leading. In my inner man I knew that I was being drawn to a radical move across the country. Jesus was asking me if I would step out of the boat and launch into the unknown. As with any would-be step of faith, I was uncertain about some things. My natural mind was spinning rapidly, but my inner man was resolute the entire time. This was not just an idea or feeling. This was indeed heavenly planning unfolding.

Jesus sometimes gave instructions that made no sense in the natural:

> When He had finished speaking, He said to Simon, "Launch out into the deep and let down your nets for a catch." Simon answered Him, "Master, we have worked all night and have caught nothing. But at Your word I will let down the net."
>
> —LUKE 5:4–5

This instruction from Jesus to Simon was one example. Simon and his team had been toiling all night with no results. Why in the world would they go back out into the same waters and expect a different result? Plus Jesus was asking them to go out even further. This is a prophetic picture. Many of the great turning points in our lives begin with what appears to be a crazy instruction. This is why we must come into proper understanding of who we are and how we were created. Every fiber of our being is designed for the supernatural! We were never intended to live our lives within the shackles of limitation. We were created for the launch into the unknown. We were created for radical kingdom exploits and breakthrough living.

Jesus's instruction challenged the natural thinking of Simon. It did not make any sense for him to obey this command. If he had asked all the "experts" in the fishing business of the day, they would have told him that he was wasting his time. It seemed to be a fruitless journey, but it was in fact the gateway to a twofold miracle—the same type of miracles God wants to accomplish in our lives by teaching us how to receive His downloads and walk in His insight. When Simon obeyed Jesus's instruction, there was such a great harvest that their nets could not handle it:

> When they had done this, they caught a great number of fish, and their net was tearing. So they signaled to their partners in the other boat to come and help them. And they came and filled both boats, so that they began to sink. When Simon Peter saw it, he fell down at Jesus' knees, saying, "Depart from me, for I am a sinful man, O Lord." For he and all who were with him were astonished at the catch of fish which they had taken.
>
> —LUKE 5:6–9

One simple word from God can unlock overwhelming blessings.

The twofold miracle was this: provision and deeper relationship. God is not a natural person. He does not live in this limited earthly realm. He is a supernatural being. We, as His children, are created to be supernatural people. Communication from the heavenly realm should be totally normal. Supernatural encounters often prick the hearts of men, convincing them of the reality of the power of God Almighty. Simon Peter had an overwhelming harvest, but he also had such a deep encounter with God that he ended up on his knees.

RADICAL RISKS BRING RESULTS

Supernatural living will produce a pattern of great surrender. The more that we see God move in our lives and experience the results of His leading, the deeper our dependency and sense of longing for Him grows. There is another layer of this story. When they could not handle the overwhelming harvest, they had to call for their partners. Our obedience, or lack thereof, has lasting consequences. We can move so far in the blessing of God that our family, friends, and people around us are affected. Hearing the voice of God, discovering the path for our lives, and taking the plunge pays huge dividends that will greatly bless others.

This is what happened in my own life. I took a radical risk of faith that made no sense in the natural. I followed the leading to go to Bible college all the way across the nation. I was on a journey that would challenge me to my very core! God was going to rip things away that the enemy had placed on my life. He was going to add the deep things of the Spirit and teach me how to be His child. That single decision still reverberates in my life today. My family was blessed because I chose to launch out into the deep. My whole life shifted course based upon a seemingly simple direction that had profound consequences. Was it easy? No way! Did it make sense in the natural? Absolutely not. Was there sacrifice? Tremendous. Was it worth it? I wouldn't trade it for the world.

This series of events began with what I call an inner witness. We will explore that concept further in a later chapter. Simply put, it is your spirit man responding to the will of God. Something on the inside reacts to the plans of heaven. In my case it was divine excitement. My spirit man was so connected to what I was hearing and the plans for my future that I was leaping inside. I did not have a dramatic word, just a leading.

Many believers have more faith in the ability of the enemy to deceive them than in their own ability to hear from God. We must understand that hearing from heaven is not something that we do but rather a part of who we are. To illustrate this, picture a satellite receiver. A satellite receiver is designed to receive communication from the primary satellite. You do not have to constantly worry about whether or not it will receive communication. It was made to do just that. You simply connect it to your devices and voilà, there it is—broadcast received, data relayed. There is clear communication without disruption because that is what it was created for.

In his book *Hosting the Presence* Bill Johnson says, "Every believer is aware of God, but not always at a conscious level."[1] Developing this awareness is one of the most important aspects of our life in Christ. He is called "God with us" (Matt. 1:23). Knowing Him that way is essential to our development.

This is the reality of our calling. We are called to abide in Him. Part of that abiding is becoming aware of His systems of communication and the fact that revelation is our birthright as children of God. The Father has laid out a unique and blessed path for each one of us; it is our privilege to discover every step. Not only that, but His voice creates light upon the path so we clearly see the way and navigate forward. We are to live lives that are in sync with the thoughts and intents of our Father's heart. We are to be planted fully and deeply in Him without shame or fear.

YOUR NEW NATURE HEARS THE VOICE

Part of our new nature as believers is a redeemed spirit man that looks like our Father. Our spirit man is created to receive continual communication from the realm of heaven. Our spirit man dwells in the realm of the spirit and is called to subdue and conquer the natural realm with the power of the kingdom.

Scripture calls us the temple of God. "Do you not know that you are the temple of God, and that the Spirit of God dwells in you?" (1 Cor. 3:16). We read things like this and then go right back to our natural way of thinking, yet there is profound revelation in this single verse. Let's start with what a temple is. According to *Webster's*, one definition of a temple is "a place devoted to a special purpose."[2] Think on this for a moment. God calls us temples. We are people created for a special purpose. We are living containers. We are born in the image of God and created to manifest His kingdom. We are called to be living, breathing, walking containers of glory. What happens if a container gets too full? It spills out! This should be the picture of our lives; we are so in tune with God that He is spilling out of us everywhere.

Just as Peter walked down the road and people were healed by his shadow, so should our lives be entry points for the kingdom of God (Acts 5:15–16). As we learn to tap into our new nature and listen to the inner conversation, we become purveyors of power and governors of glory! What do I mean by that? I mean that the very voice of God unlocks realms of power and authority in our lives that suppress the kingdom of darkness and release the strength of heaven.

If we could come to a place of realizing how much the Lord has done in our creation as new beings, we would be positioned so much further in the things of the spirit. Instead we are often held back and unnecessarily hindered. Our spirit man likes what God likes and dislikes what God dislikes. Our spirit man does not have bad days and good days but is continually filled with the power of God. The issue is that the natural realm has often become more real to us than the spirit realm. But there is a new nature inside of us! Read what Scripture says:

> But you did not learn about Christ in this manner, if indeed you have heard Him and have been taught by Him, as the truth is in Jesus: that you put off the former way of life in the old nature, which is corrupt according to the deceitful lusts, and be renewed in the spirit of your mind; and that you put on the new nature, which was created according to God in righteousness and true holiness.
>
> —EPHESIANS 4:20–24

There is a spirit nature that craves the presence of God. There is an inner peace and dominion that came the minute we were born again. A new nature describes an entirely different way of living and thinking. We are no longer people who just do what we want or feel in the moment. We are people who intend to understand and navigate the will of God. Part of that nature is spiritual communication. God's voice empowers us to obey Him. We hear and we respond.

One of the weapons of the enemy is to blind us to the realm of the spirit. This is not only an individual attack but also a corporate attack. If Satan can mute our hearing and dull our seeing, then he can rob the benefits of spirit leading. If Simon Peter had not clearly heard and obeyed Jesus's instruction to launch out, he would have never enjoyed the harvest or the encounter that came after he obeyed. As the Gospel of John reads, many people are living their lives in spiritual blindness: "He has blinded their eyes and hardened their hearts, lest they should see with their eyes and perceive with their hearts and turn, and I would heal them" (John 12:40).

There is a heart connection that happens when we see and hear in the spirit. This is part of our new nature: revelation. We unlock miracles and breakthroughs by revelation. As we discover God's insight and wisdom, we are divinely equipped for exploits. This is not the language of the mind; it is the language of the inner man. Notice that the scripture from John speaks of the eyes and the heart. There is a powerful connection between prophetic leading and inner believing.

The Gospel of Matthew records Jesus talking about those who do not have the ability to see or hear in the realm of the spirit:

> Therefore I speak to them in parables: "Because they look, but do not see. And they listen, but they do not hear, neither do they understand." In them is fulfilled the prophecy of Isaiah which says: "By hearing, you will hear and shall not understand, and seeing, you will see and shall not perceive; for this people's heart has grown dull. Their ears have become hard of hearing, and they have closed their eyes, lest they should see with their eyes and hear with their ears and understand with their hearts, and turn, and I should heal them." But blessed are your eyes, for they see, and your ears, for they hear.
>
> —MATTHEW 13:13–16

Jesus was unable to unfold truth to them in its fullness because their spiritual eyes could not see and spiritual ears could not hear. This is not the condition of someone who has been born again. When you have been brought into the kingdom, you have been brought into alignment with the voice of the Lord. Your spiritual senses have been activated. You are not called to stumble around in the darkness but to live in the light of God's revealed voice.

GOD'S VOICE BRINGS CLARITY

Before Paul came into the kingdom, he was known as Saul, a violent persecutor of the early church. He aggressively fought against the advancement of the gospel. He was bound by religious spirits and mired in deception. He could not hear the voice of the Lord. Deception creates wrong direction. This is one of the many reasons we need to be in tune with the voice of God. We need insight to continue down the right path and stay in tune with the Father.

Paul was traveling down the road to Damascus when the Lord knocked him down to the ground and supernaturally broke the spirit of deception off him. The voice of the Lord spoke to him. This is what the voice of the Lord does: it cuts right to the heart of the matter and brings the power of God on the scene. Paul needed to be delivered from religious deception. The voice of the Lord brought freedom to him on that road, and he was never the same. When God speaks, there is great clarity and freedom. The glorious light of God was shining so bright all around Paul that his physical eyes were blinded. (See Acts 9.) Though this was a physical problem, I believe it was a spiritual picture. Paul was set free, but it would take heavenly vision and prophetic revelation to propel him into the destiny of God for his life. Illumination would bring transformation to him. The scales needed to fall from his eyes. This is a picture of many people in this hour. They have been freed from the bondage of sin and pain, yet they are stumbling around frustrated. Why are they so irritated? I believe because they are living outside their purpose. When you are not doing what you were created to do, there is a deep unsettled feeling. This is what many people live with every day. The reality is that as a child of God your purpose should be one of the most natural things for you. God causes you to become aware of why you exist, what problems you were created to solve, and what victories you were born to enjoy.

When Paul's eyes were opened, he immediately began preaching the truth:

> Then Ananias went his way and entered the house. Putting his hands on him, he said, "Brother Saul, the Lord Jesus, who appeared to you on the way as you came, has sent me so that you may see again and be filled with the Holy Spirit." Immediately something like scales fell from his eyes, and he could see again. And he rose up and was baptized. When he had eaten, he was strengthened. For several days Saul was with the disciples in Damascus. Immediately he preached in the synagogues that the Christ is the Son of God.
>
> —Acts 9:17–20

As Paul's vision came forth, he was released into his assignment. Our ability to clearly see in the spirit directly impacts our recognition and fulfillment of our life's mission. As Paul advanced in his apostolic calling, he became a man of revelation. He received insight to write nearly two-thirds of the New Testament as he consistently spent time with God and learned to live tuned in. In fact, he became so aware of the absolute necessity of spiritual insight that it became one of his major prayer focuses for his spiritual sons and daughters:

> Therefore I also, after hearing of your faith in the Lord Jesus and your love toward all the saints, do not cease giving thanks for you, mentioning you in my prayers, so that the God of our Lord Jesus Christ, the Father of glory, may give you the Spirit of wisdom and revelation in the knowledge of Him, that the eyes of your understanding may be enlightened, that you may know what is the hope of His calling and what are the riches of the glory of His inheritance among the saints, and what is the surpassing greatness of His power toward us who believe, according to the working of His mighty power.
> —EPHESIANS 1:15–19

Paul stated to the church at Ephesus that he was in a state of continual prayer for them. This is evidence of his deep and abiding love for them. These words continue to reverberate as they are read today. The prayer of Paul contains insight into successful Christian living. What was one of his top prayer requests for his sons and daughters? He prayed for the spirit of wisdom and revelation to be activated in the lives of the Ephesians.

This is a prayer that is so relevant to every believer. We need heavenly guidance, insight, and leading in our daily lives. Paul was praying a very strategic prayer that we can use as a road map and a confession to declare over our own lives. We should take this prayer and pray it over ourselves as a part of our spiritual strategy.

Paul's choice of words is vital. According to the *KJV New Testament Greek Lexicon*, the Greek word here for *wisdom* means "knowledge and intelligence; knowledge of diverse matters, which includes the act of interpreting dreams and skill in management of affairs; and supreme intelligence such as belongs to God."[3] There are so many layers here. This prayer is a gateway into our true identities. We, as children of God, have complete access to God's intelligence. As we ask for the spirit of wisdom, we are laying claim to the mind of the all-knowing One with total understanding and comprehension. Paul would not pray for something that was not possible! This is not only possible; this is part of the grace for heavenly downloads. These glimpses into the mind of God take the lid off our own human understanding and access the full spectrum of God's infinite knowledge. In a moment our being is flooded with guidance and wisdom. The understanding of dreams is part of the spirit of wisdom. (Dreams will be discussed further later in the book.)

The word for *revelation* here is a Greek word that means "laying bare, making naked" and "disclosure of truth, instruction concerning things that were unknown."[4] The spirit of revelation peels back the layers to expose what is beneath the surface. It is like radar vision in the spirit. We are able to see what we previously could not see and know that which was unknown. Again, this is all established in our birthright and in who we are called to be.

This is one of my favorite passages about hearing from heaven:

> For as many as are led by the Spirit of God, these are the sons of God. For you have not received the spirit of slavery again to fear. But you have received the Spirit

of adoption, by whom we cry, "Abba, Father." The Spirit Himself bears witness with our spirits that we are the children of God, and if children, then heirs: heirs of God and joint-heirs with Christ, if indeed we suffer with Him, that we may also be glorified with Him.

—ROMANS 8:14–17

This scripture unveils the concept of insight from the position of sonship. In other words, we should be receiving heavenly communication on a daily basis because of who we are. We were delivered from a place of striving and earning to a place of dwelling and receiving. We were removed from a concept of servanthood and placed in a position of family and sonship. We are no longer in the outer courts looking in. We are in the inner courts, at the King's table as His kids. Everything about us is planted in the royalty of heaven.

This is how we stand in confidence knowing that we can and will receive from the voice of our Father. He has created us to hear His voice above all the static!

In discovering and securing our place of supernatural hearing and seeing, we must recognize the strong instructions of Jesus, just as sheep recognize the shepherd's voice:

When he brings out his own sheep, he goes before them. And the sheep follow him, for they know his voice. Yet they will never follow a stranger, but will run away from him. For they do not know the voice of strangers.

—JOHN 10:4–5

The enemy does his very best to raise objections to these types of promises. He disqualifies us with fear, with shame, with a perceived lack of experience, and with any other lie he can throw at us. We need to fix our hearts and minds in the reality of the power of the new creation and who we are in Him. The strongest voice we should hear is that of the Father. The voices of others should be greatly diminished in our lives.

A preacher friend of mine tells the story of people coming to her and asking for prayer because they were struggling to hear God's voice. She says that they would often state that the enemy was telling them that they don't hear from God. Her point is the false thought process in this request. These individuals are absolutely confident that they are hearing the devil as he tells them they can't hear from God, but they are totally unsure of their ability to hear God. This is a fallacy perpetuated from hell itself to deceive the believer. We are born, created, and wired to hear from heaven on a regular basis.

#Prayer

Father, I pray for the spirit of wisdom and revelation in our lives. I pray that the eyes of our inner man are open and we see in the realm of the spirit. I pray for a fresh perspective on who we are and our identity in the Father. I claim supernatural understanding, hidden things being revealed, and the mind of Christ in operation in our daily lives, in Jesus's name.

#Prophecy

I see a watchtower or observation point in the spirit. The Lord is teaching you how to climb in prayer and gain heavenly perspective! He is releasing divine insight, input, and revelation.

#Activation

Read Paul's prayer in Ephesians 1 and make it personal! Call forth wisdom and revelation in your own life. Take each point and apply it to yourself. Make this a spiritual prescription for seemingly blocked hearing and seeing.

#Inheritance #Hardwired #DivineCommunication

CHAPTER 2

WAYS GOD SPEAKS

· · · · · · · · · · · · · · · ·

Access to the Revelation of Heaven

ONCE WE ARE born again, we are firmly established in the family of God. The redemptive work of Jesus crushed and defeated the powers of hell, releasing us to the fullness of expression as the sons and daughters of the living God. There is perhaps no greater evidence of our complete redemption than the great privilege of being invited to access all the revelation heaven has for us. God has created us to flow in the know! He does not withhold His instructions, His thoughts, or His ideas from His kids. On the contrary, He boldly invites us to discover who He is and how He functions.

Oftentimes we fail to recognize the journey of discovery. The voice of God has many facets and methods of communication. It can be like a beautiful ball of yarn waiting to be unraveled and woven into the tapestry of our lives. One moment God shows us a piece of information through a dream. The next moment He speaks through an idea and then later possibly through something we see on a billboard. The truth is that God is always talking. We just have to learn to pursue.

I was on an airplane once when the Lord instructed me to give a word of knowledge to the guy sitting next to me. He was amazed because God revealed a deep desire that he had, and through me God spoke to this man's potential. When the plane landed, the Lord told me to leave immediately. The man was asking me other questions, so I was shocked at how the Lord prompted me to leave without answering them. I later asked the Lord why, and He told me that He wanted the man left with some mystery. I still didn't understand, but the Lord showed it to me: mystery can unlock pursuit. God does not hide Himself from us; He reserves Himself for us. The mystery of His voice is unlocked by pursuit. Our lives are to be living expressions of the pursuit of God.

When God speaks, He uses a variety of methods of communication. His voice is not in a fixed and locked position coming into our lives in only one way. There is a multiplicity of ways that He can speak to us. Our spirit man is the receiver, and He is the sender. It is vital that we position ourselves for the downloads of heaven. We must learn to rightly discover and discern His voice. It can be very easy to overlook a spirit leading if we do not recognize the various means of communication.

GOD SPEAKS THROUGH HIS WORD

I meet so many people who are sincerely struggling to recognize God's direction for their lives. They are willing to read a thousand books, attend seminars, and travel great distances just to get equipped to hear God's voice, but one of the most fundamental ways that God speaks to His people and leads them is through His written Word.

Every prophetic person must begin with the reality that God's voice never goes against His Word. The written Word of God is the basis for prophetic communication, personal knowledge, and spiritual guidance. It would greatly sharpen the prophetic sword of the body of Christ if we would train people to develop a sincere passion for the Word of God!

We are encouraged to desire the pure milk of the Word of God like a baby craves the nutrients and sustenance of milk: "As newborn babies, desire the pure milk of the word, that by it you may grow" (1 Pet. 2:2). Our prophetic foundation needs to be in the Word of God. I am mortified when I witness ministers who are well respected in prophetic circles share something that is completely contrary to the Word of God. I have even been challenged by ministers with large platforms and ministries who vehemently disagreed with my questioning their experience because it did not line up with the Word of God.

The truth is that a prophetic culture that is not rooted in a deep appreciation for the written Word of God quickly becomes toxic and entertains false fire. The Word of God is both a foundation for our spiritual experiences and a plumb line in helping us to determine what is real and what is false.

When you get into the arena of encounters, unusual and strange things are not the exception but the norm! Prophetic people have heavenly encounters that blow their earthly minds. Being swept up in a vision so vivid you cannot tell if you are in the earthly realm or heavenly realm can shake your human intellect.

Paul described the wild realm of dreams and visions:

> Doubtless it is not profitable for me to boast. So I will move on to visions and revelations of the Lord. I knew

a man in Christ over fourteen years ago—whether in the body or out of the body I cannot tell, God knows— such a one was caught up to the third heaven. And I knew that such a man—whether in the body or out of the body I cannot tell, God knows—was caught up into paradise and heard inexpressible words not permitted for a man to say.

—2 CORINTHIANS 12:1–4

One friend of mine calls these types of encounters "prophetic swirls." It is like being swept up into a prophetic whirlwind where you are in between the two worlds. This is actually a fairly normal occurrence for a person who is active in prophetic encounters.

The reality is that all of these experiences should agree with the Word of God. God is never going to tell a person something in a prophecy, a dream, or a vision that contradicts His Word. We should always use the written Word of God to rightly discern a prophetic experience or leading. The problem is that you cannot rightly discern by the Word if you have not been diligent to study and dive deep into the Scripture. This is why prophetic people must invest quality time into reading, meditating on (praying and pondering), and studying the Word of God.

Scripture talks of the importance of the Word:

In the beginning was the Word, and the Word was with God, and the Word was God. He was in the beginning with God. All things were created through Him, and without Him nothing was created that was created.

—JOHN 1:1–3

The written Word of God contains principles, teaching, spirit, and life! The Bible is not a book that is fixed in a stationary position. It is a living word that continues to grow and speak life into our hearts. It is the road map; it is the beacon of light. It is the foundation for our lives.

You must learn to go to the Word of God for direction, life, and correction. When you feel stuck and are not sure which way to go, pray and then get in the Bible. I remember a day when I was really wrestling with some decisions and what the Lord was saying to me. I couldn't seem to get any solid prophetic leading. There was no dream, no impression, no encounter. So I prayed and asked the Lord to speak to me through His Word. I opened my Bible, and words began to leap off the page and hit my spirit like a lightning bolt! I was encouraged and strengthened.

Make a practice of diving into the Word of God and reading the Bible while praying and meditating. Chew on the Word and let it hit the digestive system of your spirit. This is one of the ways God speaks. He illuminates His Word and reveals His person from the pages of your Bible. Hear the Word of God with listening ears.

THE REALM OF VISIONS AND SENSES

Another method of prophetic leading is the realm of visions. As believers we have open spiritual eyes that see and reveal heavenly communication. One of the words for *prophet* in the Old Testament is the Hebrew word *ro'eh*, and it is most commonly translated *seer*.[1] There is a dimension of spirit leading that is visual in nature. This is the realm where dreams and visions come to life. Prophetic dreams are a crucial tool in our arsenal of spirit leading and revelation, and we should not only ask for the dreams, but we should stand with confidence that God is providing to us the ability to understand what He is speaking. Many believers overlook this method of communication simply because they do not understand it. As Proverbs 20:12 says, "The hearing ear and the seeing eye, the LORD has made both of them."

There are different types of visions that a person can have:

- Open visions: This is the highest form of vision but also the least common. It is a high level of experience in which your natural eyes are wide open, yet you are swiftly caught up in the heavenly realm. Your spiritual eyes overtake your natural eyes as you begin to see things in the spiritual realm as though they are in the natural realm.

- Night vision: This is a vision that is received in the realm between consciousness and unconsciousness. In the space between sleep and wakefulness there is an encounter that holds a message. One of the primary differences between a night vision and a prophetic dream is that night visions are less symbolic and more literal, like a regular vision. They contain direction, instruction, and leading.

- Inner vision: This is a vision that takes place in the inner man. It is like a little movie playing on the inside of the spiritual mind. I have had many of these little inner visions throughout the years; many times I have viewed an entire service to know exactly what God wanted to do.

Another key to hearing from heaven is recognizing the spiritual senses. Just as in the natural realm you have senses, in the spirit realm you can receive communication through your senses. You can smell something that confirms an impure atmosphere. You can taste something that communicates discerning. You can hear a spoken word, the voice of God, communicating with you. You can see something. One of the most vivid encounters I had with the sense of smell was at an explosive revival meeting I was preaching in Canada. We were with a group of very sincere leaders who were laboring in a tough region. One night during the meeting, the fire of God showed up with such velocity that we could hardly stand up! People were encountering God with falling, weeping, trembling, and electricity. A man came up to me at the end of the meeting to tell me that he had not experienced the power of God like that in many years. As we left the building that night, we smelled smoke. Something was on fire. We looked everywhere, but there was no natural fire. It was a sign that the fire of heaven had invaded that gathering.

I have had terrible odors come into my senses at times when I was around a severely demonized person. This was simply a confirmation of what was happening in the spirit realm. We must not overlook little pictures and confirmations. When God starts speaking about something in your life, the signs will be everywhere. It is so easy to overlook these confirmations. Once I had a word burning in my spirit about the hubs the Father is establishing as centers of outpouring, and suddenly everywhere I went I would see the word *hub*. I saw it on billboards and signs and even stumbled onto a place while on vacation that was called "The Hub." At that place the Lord unfolded a powerful prophetic picture to me about His plans for the hour. All of these things were just natural things, but God used them to highlight His voice to me. Spirit leading begins with a strong inner knowing, and then there are multiple layers of confirmation. Elijah heard from God in a still, small voice:

> And after the earthquake, a fire came, but the LORD was not in the fire, and after the fire, a still, small voice.
> —1 KINGS 19:12

This still, small voice is one of the most dominant methods of heavenly conversation. There is an inner speaking that you must be quiet to hear. Many people miss this leading because they are looking for a vivid and dramatic encounter while God is nudging them on the inside. It is imperative that we make time to tune in to His voice on a daily basis.

You have spiritual eyes and ears as well as a spiritual mind. This means God speaks to you through His voice. You will hear things in your inner man. God speaks through visions, dreams, and inner pictures, but He also speaks to the mind of your spirit man. You can receive impressions, God thoughts, and subtle leadings. The realm of heavenly knowledge opens up and you suddenly know something by the Spirit. You don't know how you know, but you just know. The word of knowledge often comes to me through what I call a God thought. I suddenly have something blaze across my mind's eye, but I know it is not my own thought or idea. I have learned to recognize it as the operation of my spiritual mind. When I act upon the revelation, it opens a door to heavenly results.

God can and does speak through prophetic words. There are times in your life when you are seeking confirmation, direction, and encouragement. God may send someone to you to release a prophetic word. The prophetic ministry builds up the people of God! When you receive a prophetic word, there is a building mantle upon it to lift you up onto a higher level of understanding and living: "But he who prophesies speaks to men for their edification and exhortation and comfort" (1 Cor. 14:3).

When you receive a prophetic word, it is vital that you write or record it so that you can align your heart with it. Standing on the word of the Lord propels you forward in times of adversity and shaking. There is a supernatural strength that comes when heaven shows up and speaks to you.

A WARNING IN THE NIGHT

On many occasions I have had supernatural encounters in the night season. The Lord has unfolded instructions, assignments, and critical direction for my life through dreams and night visions. I went through a season when I woke up before sunrise many days as the Lord was speaking to me. It was one of my favorite times; I received countless downloads that continue to provide strength, even now. I have learned to pay attention to dreams. Do not shrug off a vivid dream just because you do not have the interpretation or because it doesn't seem to be overtly spiritual. There are often vital details to be uncovered just beneath the surface. This is one of the key things to understand about unraveling mysteries—it requires searching, seeking, and knocking. As the psalmist kept seeking, so should you:

Hear, O LORD, when I cry with my voice! Be gracious
to me and answer me. When You said, "Seek My face,"
my heart said to You, "Your face, LORD, I will seek."
—PSALM 27:7–8

Many people simply give up before they "crack the code."
They have a dream that seems so real, so vivid, and it stands
out to them when they wake up, but they don't understand it.
There are people who have erroneously taught that dreams
are a lower level of spiritual communication. I can remember
hearing certain teachers and ministers proclaim that the
only reason for a prophetic dream is because you were not
tuned in during the day. They devalued this form of spiritual communication and unknowingly hindered the prophetic destiny of a generation. This is how the enemy works:
he sows lies to derail powerful kingdom plans and purposes.
But the Lord greatly values the ministry of dreams:

He said, "Hear now My word. If there is a prophet
among you, I the LORD will make Myself known to
him in a vision, and I will speak to him in a dream."
—NUMBERS 12:6

It is in our dreams that we fly, climb huge mountains, go
on great adventures, and confront seemingly insurmount-
able opposition. There are no limits in the world of dreams!
Natural laws do not apply, and symbols, pictures, and experiences come alive in full view. Dreams can become platforms for next-level heavenly communication and insight.

There are three common elements of a prophetic dream:

- Instruction: When the Lord speaks to you in a
  dream, there is often a release of heavenly wisdom.

This is what I love about downloads—they contain next-level insight. You are equipped on a greater level.

• Revelation: There is illumination in godly dreams. The spotlight shines upon situations, opportunities, and relationships. God knows *everything*. When He speaks to you, you are brought to a higher level of information and understanding. You can suddenly see what you could not see before.

• Direction: Dreams are often used as tools to communicate an assignment, new relationship, or transition. Many times a dream will provide reinforcement of a particular direction or unveil a stunning new roadway.

In *Dreams and Visions: Understanding and Interpreting God's Messages to You*, Jane Hamon wrote:

> *Webster's* dictionary defines a *dream* as "a succession of images or ideas present in the mind during sleep." Dreams are formed in the subconscious mind based on images and symbols that are unique to the individual, depending on his or her background, experience and current life circumstances.
>
> Dreams can communicate truth about ourselves—or others—that our conscious minds might have failed to acknowledge. One word for *dream* in the Greek language is *enupnion*, which is defined as "something seen in sleep or a vision in a dream."[2]

God used dreams to communicate with individuals in the Bible, setting a precedent for what we experience today. Let's look at Jacob and his dream:

> Then Jacob went out from Beersheba and went toward Harran. He came to a certain place and stayed there all night, because the sun had set. He took one of the stones of that place and put it under his head, and lay down in that place to sleep. He dreamed and saw a ladder set up on the earth with the top of it reaching to heaven. The angels of God were ascending and descending on it. The LORD stood above it and said, "I am the LORD God of Abraham your father and the God of Isaac. The land on which you lie, to you will I give it and to your descendants. Your descendants will be like the dust of the earth, and you will spread abroad to the west and to the east and to the north and to the south, and in you and in your descendants all the families of the earth will be blessed. Remember, I am with you, and I will protect you wherever you go, and I will bring you back to this land. For I will not leave you until I have done what I promised you."
>
> Jacob awoke out of his sleep, and he said, "Surely the LORD is in this place, and I did not know it." He was afraid and said, "How awesome is this place! This is none other but the house of God, and this is the gate of heaven."
>
> —GENESIS 28:10–17

Jacob was fleeing from his brother, Esau, when he had a profound dream. The Lord began to show him an open heaven. He revealed an entry point of angelic activity— heaven crashing down onto Earth. Jacob discovered a bethel, a dwelling place of the Lord. There are often times in our lives when we are torn about a particular decision and our spiritual vision seems blocked. No matter how much we are praying, seeking, and asking, we cannot seem to get the right answer. I think this is usually because our minds are blocking our inner man as emotions swirl. In the middle of the night God can come with a confirming dream, just as He did in the life of Jacob. As he was being threatened and attacked by his brother, God revealed angelic assistance and divine guidance and provided a heavenly encounter. Revelation is our portion. We should expect spirit encounters, God leadings, and divine interruptions.

Cracking the code

Dreams can come from a variety of sources. Let's begin by understanding that not all dreams are from God. There is a dividing line in the world of dreams. The line is the same one that applies to all revelation. It is the line of division between the soul and the spirit.

> For the word of God is alive, and active, and sharper than any two-edged sword, piercing even to the division of soul and spirit, of joints and marrow, and able to judge the thoughts and intents of the heart.
>
> —HEBREWS 4:12

The word of God brings definition to what is coming from the soul (mind, will, and emotions) and what is coming from the realm of the spirit.

Dreams from the soul

Dreams can originate from your own mind. They can be like movies telling a story of a memory, desire, trauma, pain, or ambition. You can have a very peaceful dream that is from your own mind. Typically dreams from the soul have no real sense of profound urgency. They don't strike you as having a significant message even though they may have been extremely vivid.

Dreams from the spirit: the enemy

The other realm that dreams come from is the realm of the spirit. Now it is important to distinguish that spiritual dreams can be motivated by two sources: the realm of darkness and the enemy, or the kingdom of God bringing direction and heavenly communication. It is fairly easy to identify a demonic attack. We often refer to scary dreams as nightmares.

Webster's defines a *nightmare* as

1. an evil spirit formerly thought to oppress people during sleep;

2. a frightening dream that usually awakens the sleeper; and

3. something (as an experience, situation, or object) having the monstrous character of a nightmare or producing a feeling of anxiety or terror.[3]

A demonic dream is an evil message or manifestation from the realm of the spirit. There are many reasons why people are attacked in their sleep. Most people are completely unaware of something I call the law of transfer. God instructed us over and over in His Word to impart, bless, heal, and minister through the laying on of hands. Simply put, we are to release the power of the kingdom through touch.

In Jesus's final instructions before leaving Earth, He commissioned all believers to lay hands on the sick:

These signs will accompany those who believe: In My
name they will cast out demons; they will speak with
new tongues; they will take up serpents; if they drink
any deadly thing, it will not hurt them; they will lay
hands on the sick, and they will recover.

—MARK 16:17–18

The laying on of hands is one of the strong healing ministries of the body of Christ. The healing ministry is part of
the spiritual DNA of all believers. In fact, the Book of James
instructs believers struggling with infirmity to call for the
elders to anoint them with oil and release healing:

Is anyone sick among you? Let him call for the elders
of the church, and let them pray over him, anointing
him with oil in the name of the Lord. And the prayer
of faith will save the sick, and the Lord will raise
him up. And if he has committed any sins, he will be
forgiven.

—JAMES 5:14–15

We can look back to the Old Testament and see the ministry of the laying on of hands for blessing and impartation.
As Moses's time was drawing to a close, God told him to
bring Joshua before him and release his anointing, strength,
and mantle to him by the laying on of hands (Num. 27:18–20).
He was able to supernaturally impart a level of authority
and grace upon him. The same is true today. There is tremendous power in association and impartation. It is imperative that we recognize the value of being connected to the
right people as well as the grave danger in being connected
to the wrong people.

The hands of a believer are mighty instruments of power.

It is amazing that you can touch someone who is being attacked and harassed by the enemy and release the peace of God!

When dealing with nightmares, remember the enemy does not create anything. He simply twists and perverts kingdom principles. Those involved in witchcraft and evil practices intentionally look to open windows in the spirit to release evil spirits and attacks. I once had someone try to give me "a gift" at a meeting, but I discerned that it was a tool. The Lord revealed to me the operation of witchcraft in the person presenting the object to me. I immediately had a sense that I was not to take it. That might seem crazy to you, but Scripture tells us that witchcraft has objects associated with it. The Bible records this:

> This became known to all Jews and Greeks living in Ephesus. And fear fell on them all, and the name of the Lord Jesus was magnified. Many who believed came confessing and telling their deeds. Many who practiced magic brought their books together and burned them before everyone. They calculated their value, which equaled fifty thousand drachmas. So the word of the Lord powerfully grew and spread.
>
> —ACTS 19:17–20

Ephesus was experiencing great revival, and in the midst of the move there was powerful deliverance taking place. They burned the books (objects) associated with witchcraft. Part of their advance into freedom was the shedding of things that tied them to the dark realm.

Just as we touch and release the presence of God, people with evil intent often touch you or, as I said earlier, give you something. I want to pause and interject that there is absolutely no fear in Jesus! He has provided complete freedom for you and me. There is no need for us to yield to any type of fear. We learn about demonic operations to avoid the traps of the enemy, not to empower fear.

Many times an evil dream is the result of a contact. Perhaps we were around someone with a strong spirit of lust, and then at night we had a lustful dream. The enemy will use that dream to bring condemnation and confusion. Dreams can and do originate from the realm of the spirit and are significant in our lives. One of the more common evil dreams many experience is a manifestation of fear that comes after exposing themselves to something attached to the spirit of fear. They may watch a movie about serial killers, occult practices, or evil supernatural experiences and then have a nightmare. When this happens, there was a transfer of the spirit of fear, and it needs to be broken. It is as simple as recognizing, identifying, and rising in authority to break the attack. Slam the door shut. Scripture says:

> Do not give place to the devil.
>
> —EPHESIANS 4:27

Dreams from the spirit: Holy Spirit

Dreams also come from our inner man, our born-again spirit. They come from Holy Spirit. These types of spiritual dreams contain prophetic messages. They are very seldom literal and are quite often mysterious in nature. The dream language is usually speaking in symbols.

When you have a prophetic dream, it typically feels as though it was in high definition. I am not talking about the actual colors or images, although that can be the case. (And sometimes a demonic dream is in black and white.)

However, the high definition that I am talking about is more in the experience of the dream itself. There is something more pressing about it. You often wake up having no idea what the dream means, but it stands above other dreams you have recently had. It is a louder voice with a stronger prompting. That prompting is the first clue to crack the code.

When you awake and sense you have had a significant dream that may be prophetic in nature, it is important to write down as much detail as you possibly can. That is assignment number one. You cannot interpret what you have not recorded.

The next thing you must do is pray. Too many people rush to interpret a dream. I understand completely because there is a sense of excitement and urgency. Realize that if God thought the message was that important to send to you, you should value proper interpretation. The right dream with the wrong interpretation can give way to error. All prophetic leadings are invitations to prayer.

After praying over the details, begin to search out the meaning of the symbols. This is one of the master keys to cracking the code of dream language. Dream language speaks in symbols and pictures. These pictures are often backed up by biblical understanding, although there are times that the symbols or pictures have more to do with your own personality. When you cannot find a meaning that is clear from Scripture, it could be a personal symbol. For example, houses often represent ministries in biblical context, but if a person grew up in a particular house and dreamed about that place, it could represent a personal place of safety or protection. This is an example of a personal symbolic leading that may not be clear cut.

Do not just do a quick online search that may take you

to some New Age website. You need biblical references to properly understand what the pictures, objects, and symbols in your dream may represent. There are a variety of amazing books and websites that are dedicated to the biblical language of dreams. These are good tools. You can also do a search of the Bible itself. For example, if you dream of being submerged in crystal clear water and you wake up knowing that it is a prophetic dream, you could immediately find two possible meanings in Scripture. First, water often represents the flow of Holy Spirit:

> On the last and greatest day of the feast, Jesus stood and cried out, "If anyone is thirsty, let him come to Me and drink. He who believes in Me, as the Scripture has said, out of his heart shall flow rivers of living water." By this He spoke of the Spirit, whom those who believe in Him would receive. For the Holy Spirit was not yet given, because Jesus was not yet glorified.
> —JOHN 7:37–39

Water can also represent the Word of God:

> …that He might sanctify and cleanse it with the washing of water by the word.
> —EPHESIANS 5:26

In this example the dream about water could be an instruction that you need to dive deeper into the Word to overcome a problem or break through an obstacle. It could also be a prophetic instruction about a need for a richer life in the Spirit. Or it could be a word about something that is getting ready to happen that will expose you to a stronger flow of Holy Spirit. If this dream is not properly interpreted, then you will miss the message.

Once you have gotten some possible meanings for the symbols in your dream, it is time to go back to prayer. Begin to ponder the various possibilities while praying and asking the Lord for clear understanding. If you continue to pursue, you will crack the code and receive the message. Sometimes the Lord may even send someone with the interpretation. Always remember that every word of the Lord and every instruction is simply another opportunity to partner with the Lord in prayer. The life of the Spirit is one of prayer.

A simple warning dream

Once a very unexpected door was put before my wife and me. My first reaction was, "This is not for us." As I continued to pray and seek the Lord for guidance, my heart began to open toward the door. We have lived our entire lives in radical pursuit of the will of God. If this unexpected door was of the Lord, then I wanted to walk through it with zeal, tenacity, and integrity. I decided to take the plunge and navigate into the unknown.

A dear intercessor and mentor in our lives was deeply concerned. She knew that we were moving in rapid acceleration and did not want to see any missteps. She told us that she was praying that if the doorway was not of the Lord, then it would slam shut! We agreed.

"And we know that God causes all things to work together for good to those who love God, to those who are called according to *His* purpose" (Rom. 8:28, NASB). In its proper context this verse is a phenomenal promise. It comes right after strong instructions regarding prayer. Yielding over to prayer in the spirit opens the door for divine direction. God is literally behind the scenes arranging each and every detail for your ultimate good. We were holding on to this promise.

We kept moving forward, through the door, and I left for a ministry trip. While I was gone, my wife called me and began to relate to me a strange dream she had. She dreamed that I texted her to tell her that I had been in an accident. I told her that my cheeks were hurt but overall I was OK. The dream did not seem very profound or meaningful, yet as she related it to me, I knew there was something to it. This is one of the keys to unlocking prophetic dreams. As with any other type of spiritual communication, you must follow that inner witness, that subtle nudging down deep inside your spirit man. I knew that the dream was prophetic and we needed to dig into it. We began to research what cheeks represent in a dream and discovered that they can represent persecution, opposition, and accusation. I continued praying and seeking God for His ultimate best.

A day or so later there was a series of events, and the door that had been opened was unexpectedly slammed shut as there was a release of demonic activity. When I was informed of what was going on, I texted my wife. Later that day we talked about it in detail and felt an immediate sense of divine direction and protection over our lives. I hung up the phone with her, and all of a sudden her dream came before me. My cheeks were hurt, but I was OK. The enemy released both opposition and accusation, but the word of the Lord had already gone forth. Just as in my wife's dream, I texted her first thing. I was blown away by the goodness of the Lord and the faithfulness of His voice. Recognizing the significance of that dream brought forth revelation, instruction, and direction. God dispatched tremendous comfort and guidance to us through a simple dream. The next day

I went on a long prayer walk, and the Lord immediately began to reassure my heart that what seemed like an attack was actually protection. This closed door catapulted me into a refreshing and divine new season; it was a powerful demonstration of the protection and leading of the Lord.

#Prayer

I *decree* supernatural spirit leading—divine interruptions and sudden explosions of revelation—in our lives. I pray for powerful prophetic dreams—blessed, sweet sleep and heavenly encounters. Father, I pray our spiritual eyes and ears would be open. Let us be led by the Spirit and moving in revelation, in Jesus's name.

#Prophecy

I hear the Lord saying: "It's a time of prophetic activation, the release of seeing and knowing. There is a higher level of authoritative decree coming forth. I am teaching My people how to receive My word and then partner with it in prayer—to give birth to My promise. This is part of the fullness of My plans: knowing, seeing, receiving, waiting (not passively). I am teaching My people how to *look* into the spirit realm and see clearly. They will not see dimly, but clearly. I am elevating the level of prophetic decree coming forth. There is a governing mantle coming forth in this group. There is a divine unfolding of wisdom and revelation."

#Activation

I challenge you to take a set period of time, the next fourteen days, and pray each night thanking the Lord for prophetic dreams and sweet sleep. Keep something by your bed to write on and record anything, no matter how small. Look for those dreams that stand out or that seem to be "high definition" in nature and capture them. Use the methods I have laid out and see what the Lord is saying. Activate, expect, and pray!

#Dreamers #SpiritLed #Revelation

CHAPTER 3

STEWARD THE VOICE

· · · · · · · · · · · · · · · · ·

Created to be Creative

A S HUMAN BEINGS we are created to experience, process, and learn in a variety of ways. We have not been created with only one sense. We experience life through a multifaceted set of senses. We feel things deeply. We are impacted greatly by visual stimulation. We are often inspired and motivated to action by the words of a great orator. A stunning landscape can spark creativity in a way that perhaps no other experience can. The full harnessing of our emotional and spiritual faculties is key to becoming spiritually in tune. We must learn to accept revelation in all its various forms, and also to cultivate atmospheres and methods of prophetic acceleration.

Building surroundings that alert your prophetic senses and release your mind to dream can be a great tool in your spiritual growth. In his book *Prophetic Activation* best-selling author John Eckhardt writes, "The value of different activations is that they will break the limitations and give you the ability to operate in different ways. Don't be limited to your favorite way, but move in different ways and administrations. The prophetic anointing must never become boring and routine but should always be exciting and new. God has many surprises for us, and the prophetic anointing will always release new things."[1]

It is my belief the very nature of God Himself is creative. The very first verse in the Bible identifies the imaginative side of God: "In the beginning God created the heavens and the earth" (Gen. 1:1). In the beginning God *created*! He fulfilled a dream. God executed a plan. He manifested an imagination.

A study of the nature of God reveals His extravagant, creative personality. The throne room is not a quiet place with simple surroundings, but one filled with smoke, living creatures, and remarkable glory.

> In the year that King Uzziah died I saw the Lord sitting on a throne, high and lifted up, and His train filled the temple. Above it stood the seraphim. Each one had six wings. With two he covered his face, and with two he covered his feet, and with two he flew. One cried to another and said: "Holy, holy, holy, is the LORD of Hosts; the whole earth is full of His glory." The posts of the door moved at the voice of him who cried, and the house was filled with smoke.
>
> —ISAIAH 6:1–4

God celebrates beauty and creates extravagantly. The tabernacle was built with great specificity and abundant artistry. Nothing was simple or plain. Nothing was left to chance. God gave extremely detailed instructions because the form mattered to Him. He is at heart a creative personality with great appreciation for sight and sound. Consider the atmosphere described in the throne room as recorded in the Book of Revelation:

Immediately I was in the Spirit. And there was a throne set in heaven with One sitting on the throne! And He who sat there appeared like a jasper and a sardius stone. There was a rainbow around the throne, appearing like an emerald. Twenty-four thrones were around the throne. And I saw twenty-four elders sitting on the thrones, clothed in white garments. They had crowns of gold on their heads. Lightnings and thunderings and voices proceeded from the throne. Seven lamps of fire were burning before the throne, which are the seven Spirits of God.

—REVELATION 4:2–5

The throne room is described as a place of extreme visual beauty with the appearance of gemlike colors and the rainbow. God has a heavenly light show. There are crowns of gold unlike anything seen in the earth. There are thunders (sound) and lightning (sight) proceeding from the midst of the glory. The atmosphere around the presence of God is filled with creativity that fascinates every known sense. God is grandiose in His expression. He goes all out! He is in no way boring or plain.

Creativity is one of the manifestations of the nature of God in our lives. We are all creating something on a daily basis. When we profess failure and despair, we are creating something. When we design and decorate a special place of reflection in our homes, we are creating a place to be inspired and to dream. When we plan a much-needed vacation, we are creating a place of rest for our minds and bodies. Everything that we do is an extension of some form of creativity.

Nothing is ever created without someone first imagining it. If you can see it (in your mind's eye), you can achieve it.

Our imagination is the very center of creativity. Someone can simply tell us to imagine a tropical climate with warm white sands and calm emerald waters, and immediately we can see a beautiful beach. If we close our eyes and focus in hard, we will begin to feel a calming peace as our mind plays for us the sounds of the gentle waves lapping the smooth sandy shore. This is the power of imagination. Imagination is where sins and failures begin, along with breathtaking victories and thrilling exploits. The enemy works to overwhelm our minds with negative information while the Lord desires to assist us in renewing our minds so that our creative juices start flowing with heavenly ambition.

Many people are trapped in a deep pit of despair and hopelessness. They are in a prison so strong that no matter how much they struggle, they cannot seem to break free. The bars are strong, the gates locked, and the guards abundant. This prison is not one that has been constructed with concrete and steel, and the bars are not made of gray metal. This fortress exists in their hearts and minds. The systematic pollution and destruction of the creative imagination builds cells that are seemingly impenetrable within human minds. Yet God, in all of His power and by His living Word, holds the keys to break every human loose from the prison of mental bondage!

The prophetic spirit is a creative spirit. Prophetic experiences pull back the shade on the window into the supernatural and allow us to see what is to come. Prophetic words are living expressions of potential and possibility. Prophetic utterances are not fixed in a locked position but are alive with opportunity.

Creativity moves outside of the box, colors outside of the lines, and sees a solution where others only see problems.

Creativity can see the potential. Creative people are not limited to the normal rules and boundaries of thinking and living. They see, feel, and experience in HD. This is a common thread between creatives and prophetic people. Prophetic senses allow you to see, feel, hear, and know things from another dimension. To move prophetically, you must take the plunge off the high dive and be risky! You must be daring enough to believe what God is saying and go for it. The element of creativity is necessary to embrace and steward prophetic words. Creative atmospheres give birth to prophetic expression. Creative people partner with the unseen and take note of what God is saying.

WRITE THE VISION

Learning to properly steward the revelation of prophetic spirits is an important key to being able to act on God's word to you. Many times a single dream, vision, or inner leading will unlock the door to the wisdom of God. There are obstacles standing in the way of breakthroughs and blessings in our lives that will not be moved without tapping into the mind of God. I have found that dreams many times are the beginning of a word of wisdom.

A word of wisdom as mentioned in 1 Corinthians 12 is a divine release of the wisdom of God in a situation (v. 8). When wisdom shows up, solutions show up; when wisdom is unfolded, instruction is released. Wisdom can unlock major advances. Many times God will give us a prophetic dream to speak to us about a coming season or opportunity, but we need to pray and begin to tap the wisdom of God when we have the dream. It is one thing to know that something is coming, but it is an entirely different matter to know what to do when the opportunity arrives. As the proverb says, "Through wisdom is a house built, and by understanding it is established" (Prov. 24:3).

A friend once taught me a critical prophetic lesson. I would often receive little tidbits of insight during prayer, sometimes only a sentence or two. I would feel like those were insignificant and would not do anything with them. My friend gave me a word of wisdom and told me that I needed to write each one down and revisit them in prayer. As I began to do that, I received life-giving instructions. Many times what began as a small nugget turned into a major supernatural encounter.

You simply cannot partner with what you are not capturing!

Make a record of the revelation so that you can properly steward it. You cannot steward what you fail to record. I have come to understand that most prophetic journeys look like a road that is paved with a series of stones. Each stone has a different revelation and instruction. If you only take a single stone, you only have one step, but when you systematically piece them all together, you have a clear pathway.

One of the most basic starting points is to simply record spoken words. Since today's technology is so accessible, this is a very easy goal to achieve. If you have a smartphone or other electronic device, take it with you into your private place of prayer. When you sense something uncommon bubbling up in your spirit, be prepared to press record.

Recently I was praying when all of a sudden an unusual level of intensity hit my spirit. I had a sense that something was stirring, so I began to record. A prophetic word shot up out of my spirit, and because I recorded it, I can go back to that word over and over again as a reference. Learning to turn your prayer closet into a place of prophetic speaking, singing, and praying is a real step into the realm of the supernatural.

If you are going to a gathering, church service, or special meeting where prophetic ministry may happen, have your phone ready. Be ready to push record the moment anything is spoken over you. You will usually know at the time if it is an on-target word or not. Many times these words can propel you forward in your destiny, but you need to have them available and you need to go back to them to remind yourself of what was spoken.

To record prophetic dreams, it might be helpful to have a dream journal. Get something that inspires you, such as a notebook with a picture on the front that brings creativity forth, and keep it by your bedside. Start praying for dreams from God. You will begin to awake with vivid dreams that need prayer and interpretation. When this happens, you must write them down.

If you are a digital person like me, you can make a dream journal on your electronic device. Create a place to write down dreams. It may take days, weeks, or even months to come to the full understanding of what a dream means. Prophetic encounters are designed to unlock seeking. You must write it down, and then it can become a part of your prayer life and time with God. You are reading what you have already interpreted and praying over what needs to be interpreted.

In seasons of transition, a dream journal can be an invaluable tool. It is like a prophetic record of what God has already designed for you, and you can clearly see His handwriting in your story.

PROPHETIC IMAGES

Another realm of the prophetic is pictures and vision. For example, water is used over and over again in the Bible as a prophetic symbol. Rivers can represent the flowing of Holy Spirit. If I took a picture of a rushing river and put it in my place of prayer, I could look at it and reflect upon the potential for major moves of God. Water also represents the washing of the Word of God. The Word renews the mind and washes away unbelief and contamination.

It has been said that a picture is worth a thousand words, and I can see instances where that is true. God often speaks to me through things I see. I have prophesied based on inspiration that came through a picture. Many times my prophetic gift operates with pictures, and I see things in symbols and representation.

To record images I have seen, I have hung pictures of places on my walls or cut them out of magazines and put them on my desk for inspiration and prophetic insight. I have also downloaded images from the Internet and put them in my digital journal. Often when I write out a prophetic message, I will find a picture to go with it.

Get creative with the visual side of your prophetic personality. Put a prophetic picture on your computer as a screen saver. Make a prophetic picture scrapbook. Find pictures that go with words you have received. Don't limit your prophetic imagination. Use images that inspire the creative side of you.

DIVINE ARROWS

Prophetic words and experiences are like the tips of divine arrows. When a revelation is properly received, released,

and partnered with, it becomes a compelling weapon of war
that cuts through the assignments of the enemy! This truth
is recorded in Scripture:

> This command I commit to you, my son Timothy,
> according to the prophecies that were previously given
> to you, that by them you might fight a good fight.
> —1 TIMOTHY 1:18

In the midst of battle, Paul told his spiritual son, Timothy,
to go back to the blueprint for victory. Go back to the prophetic words that have been released over your life and arm
yourself with them. Prophetic decrees release the end of the
matter. They stand outside time and speak in the realm of
eternity. True prophetic words have the potential to invade
the natural realm with supernatural power, grace, and
authority. To be active prophetically is to be supercharged
in the spirit and empowered to win.

The Lord gave me a fourfold strategy for experiencing
supernatural victory and prophetic wisdom through the
prophetic decrees and divine arrows of the Lord:

1. Identify: What is the word of the Lord? What is
   God saying? What has already been declared?

2. Speak: Words are the creative engine of the spirit
   realm. God created by speaking what was in His
   heart. When belief meets words, supernatural
   power is released. A prophetic revelation needs
   to be declared. Declaration is a key to the dimension of creative power and authority. Believing and
   speaking are chief components of supernatural
   living.

3. Seek: Seek the instruction of the Lord. It is improper understanding to think that the matter ends because of a single revelation. The revelation was provided to open the pathway of seeking. When God speaks, there will be instruction provided to partner with the word of the Lord. Hearing and obeying the instruction is vital for supernatural results. Miracles come as the result of obeying an instruction.

4. Implement: Follow the Lord's strategy. When God provides instruction, we are responsible to execute an intentional plan. For example, if the word of the Lord is about business, then perhaps there is a sowing and preparation strategy we can follow to partner with the word of the Lord.

The enemy wants to paralyze your faith by negating your participation in the supernatural. Supernatural miracles are the result of maximized prophetic potential and human participation. This four-pronged strategy equips you for prophetic acceleration and explosive miracles.

THE IMPORTANCE OF PROPHETIC INSIGHTS

Each and every insight that God provides for you is important. The result of the revelation will often be determined by your reply and response. If you just think on it for a day or two and then let it go, you will probably miss the full effect of the oil on that word. If you write, record, and then go back to it with prayer and seeking strategy, you will keep pressing that word and extract the oil.

Different words carry different purposes. There is a

breaker realm of the prophetic that comes with real power to break down bondages. Sometimes you are struggling and need a breakthrough. God will send a word to you that contains bondage-breaking power. It may not be a word that has long-term application but is sent for that very moment.

Some words frame times and seasons. There have been times in my life that I keep pondering a word over and over, and each time I got more application. It becomes a mission statement for a season of my supernatural journey. There are other words that are very specific and hold instruction for a particular assignment.

All of these things must be prayed out and discerned. This is why recording, writing, and praying over supernatural revelations is so critical. To become a person who walks in the supernatural, you must learn to place emphasis and value on insight and revelation.

#Prayer

Thank You, Lord, for prophetic strategy and stewardship. I pray that we are becoming capable stewards of the prophetic words that are spoken over our lives. Lord, bring forth the realm of creativity and prophetic potential in our walks with You, In Jesus's name.

#Prophecy

I hear the Lord saying, "This is a time of reordering, realigning, and redefining amongst My people...Yes, I am shifting and rearranging things for My purposes and My ordination. In this hour I am releasing fresh instruction to My servants who will listen. Many have hardened both their ears and their hearts toward the things that I would say unto them because My plans may seem inconvenient to their plans. Their plans have held back My eruptions of glory, for I have strategically marked locations for eruptions of My glory…that even as a natural volcano would erupt and totally change the atmosphere, even shall My glory erupt and break forth in locations, shaking the religious foundations. But My servants must be where I tell them in order to receive what I have promised. The steps of ministry shall be reformed in this hour. Many will move into new locations, new directions—they will find themselves doing ministry in a new and different way. Churches shall receive a reordering to become centers of outpouring, not pleasing man but chasing the heart of God. Be still and sensitive in My presence as I speak, 'Arise, and run to carry forth My plans for this hour.'"

#Activation

Take a time out right now and find a prophetic picture. Just browse the Internet or find something in your house and write out two or three lines from the inspiration that comes. For example, you find a cart and write something like this: "A vessel for forward motion. The Lord is carrying me onward with destiny and grace."

Do not overcomplicate or overthink it. Tap into your inner man and loose the prophetic potential. If you can complete this activation, you are on your way to journaling and creativity in the prophetic.

#StewardMysteries #PropheticPictures

CHAPTER 4

RECEIVE INSIGHT
FROM HOLY SPIRIT

· · · · · · · · · · · · · · · ·

A Surge of Downloads

ONCE WAS ASKED by a good friend to attend a conference with some visionary leaders. This conference held special importance to me because God used the teachings of those involved to shift my life and help unlock realms of my assignment. Before the conference began, I had a fascinating dream that further confirmed the need to receive from these particular ministers. At the same time the enemy was behind the scenes doing all he could to block me from attending the event. Though many people do not properly discern this, attacks often precede kingdom surges. I am not saying that it is the case every time, but it often is. Many people simply overlook the spiritual battle, wishing and hoping it will go away. What many fail to recognize is that we have been granted authority over the enemy, but we must exercise that dominion and run on. We do not have time to be sidelined or delayed.

I pressed through the resistance, got on the plane, and headed to the conference. I was operating on about three to four hours of sleep, which is not all that unusual on travel days, but I was very groggy. I spend a lot of time writing, journaling, and studying on planes, using my electronic devices as my primary tools. I took my computer out and had it in the pocket of the seat in front of me, but I fell asleep. I was awakened by the announcement that we were landing! I gathered my things quickly and shook myself to wake up as we exited the plane. There was just one problem—I left my computer, along with hundreds of notes, articles, and other works in progress, in that pocket. By the time I realized it, the plane was gone. I never got my computer back. The distractions and warfare were all around this trip.

I made a decision to let go of the computer and focus on the gathering. The moment worship began, I was swept up in a realm of prophetic seeing. I had to type the revelations as fast as I could because the Lord was speaking to me so strongly. These revelations and prophetic words kept coming the entire time of the conference. In fact, I had three back-to-back prophetic dreams. When I asked the Lord what was happening, He told me two things. First, He told me that there is a grace and anointing (empowering force of God) for downloads. He told me to believe for prophetic downloads and make it a faith mission to function in a greater revelatory capacity. Second, He told me that it was an atmospheric thing. I had placed myself in an atmosphere with people who carry heavy levels of insight, so this pulled me up onto another level of divine seeing. The mantles unlocked my spiritual eyes and ears.

An Encounter With a Seer

I encountered a similar situation when I was gathering footage for our online television network, Awakening TV. I interviewed a prophet who is known for extremely accurate words of knowledge, such as having knowledge of names, addresses, phone numbers, and other bits of information. He was very kind, and the interview was good. I enjoyed our brief conversation. There was no prayer or any other sign of an impartation.

We left that event and headed to another city where we had a conference the next day. During worship I was suddenly and unexpectedly swept up into the revelatory realm. I knew things about people on a deeper level than I ever had before. The word of knowledge is something I operated in for many years before this; in fact, it was one of the gifts that I asked God for very early on. Through the years I have enjoyed seeing many tremendous miracles and breakthroughs by sharing tidbits of insight that God gave me. At this conference I began to give word after word about the intimate details of people's lives. This was a different level of that gift—I knew things on another dimension. The level of insight I was operating in was much higher than my normal level. I knew that even though we had not prayed together, the presence of a seer in my life had unlocked something! There is so much power in impartation and connection. Connection always unlocks flow, and sometimes we don't even realize how God is lining things up for us.

The word of knowledge is such a fascinating thing; the Lord speaks one little piece of information and you step out in faith. It is quite scary! I remember a time when I was on a plane and the man next to me was sharing his life story, but

I kept seeing another picture. What I saw made no sense at all. I thought my mind was playing tricks on me, yet I recognized the very familiar sense that this was indeed a word of knowledge. I was stumped because this guy was giving me information about himself, but what I was seeing did not go along with anything he was saying.

The reality is this: the word of knowledge and any other realm of the prophetic requires guts. Faith is a *risk*. It is just that simple. Far too many people trust their own intellect much more than their spirit man, and they never experience great miracles. Words of knowledge are like little keys that unlock doors to the dimension of power and wonders. God can give us a small and seemingly insignificant piece of information, but it swings the doors of power open wide. We must also be willing to abandon our desire to play it safe and guard our reputation. Jesus made Himself of no reputation (Phil. 2:7, KJV). He did not care what people thought of Him. The fear of man quenches the boldness of the Lord! You will not find miracles in the shallow end of the pool of the Spirit. No! Miracles are out in the deep. You must be willing to dive straight in.

Finally I overcame my struggle and just delivered the word to the man. I simply asked him if he liked to do a certain thing, and his eyes got huge! The Lord showed me a writing gift. He told me that he had been working on a book but was not sure what would come of it. He asked me how I knew these things. I shared the gospel with him and laid hands on him right there on the plane. One word opened a God-sized door!

THE PERSONHOOD OF HOLY SPIRIT

One of the challenges that we all face in our journey with God is the feeling of inadequacy, the feeling that we do not know how to do what we are being asked to do. I often tell people that I don't think I have ever known how to do what God has asked me to do. If the task was within my reach naturally, it would not require any measure of faith. The reality is that faith dwells in the realm of the unknown. Faith challenges us to move beyond our own abilities, our own knowledge, and our perceived limitations.

When Jesus walks into the temple and finds a man with a withered hand, what does He ask him to do?

> Then He said to the man, "Stretch out your hand." And he stretched it out, and it was restored whole like the other.
> —MATTHEW 12:13

It sounds so simple reading it as a story, but this event is so complex. This man lived with this crippled hand. It most likely was a source of embarrassment for him. He did not look like everyone else, nor could he do what others could do. Why would Jesus embarrass him like this? It's simple—Jesus moved beyond the realm of natural thinking. He was out in the deep and could see the man's hand healed. He just needed to stretch the man and get him out of his comfort zone.

This is what revelation often does. It moves us out past our normal realm of living and function. We are swept up in the tidal waves of glory and taken into the uncharted waters. This man could have allowed fear, embarrassment, or offense to grip him and block the miracle. These are all temptations we face when we are challenged by the Lord. Prophets are seldom concerned with human thinking and ways. When they have seen and tasted the realm of the Spirit, they are speaking from another dimension and refuse to paddle back into the shallows.

The man was given a seemingly impossible command to stretch his hand out. He could not naturally do it, and that was the whole point. The breakthrough was in the place of radical obedience. Revelation opens doors to places in the spirit that carry us far beyond our own boundaries. When the man partnered with the word of the Lord, the miracle happened.

There is another layer here to examine. The will of God for this man was healing. That was the *what*, but there was also a *how*. Revelation is the how. Many times when there is a promise to be unlocked, the key is in the *how*. The key is in tuning into Holy Spirit and letting Him direct our steps, no matter how undignified or absurd the instructions seem. Revelation swings doorways open and crushes the shackles of restriction.

The world of heavenly downloads begins with a realization of the person of Holy Spirit. Far too many times we think of the third part of the Godhead as an it. This is horrible theology. He is an actual person, as evidenced by the reality that He has thoughts, moods, emotions, and a personality. These are the complex attributes of a living being, not an inanimate object.

We are told in Ephesians 4:30 not to grieve Holy Spirit. We will dive deeper into this verse later, but it is revealing His heart. There are things we can do and say that bother Him. According to *Webster's* dictionary, the word *grieve* means "to feel sad or unhappy."[1] This expresses the emotional capacity of Holy Spirit. He has the ability to feel a particular way about situations and actions. He not only leads and guides, but He also feels.

> He who searches the hearts knows what the mind of the Spirit is, because He intercedes for the saints according to the will of God.
> —ROMANS 8:27

Praying in other tongues unlocks the mind of the Spirit. Again, we see a confirmation that Holy Spirit has a mental capacity with thoughts, feelings, and ideas. Stepping into the domain of supernatural communication means accessing the mind of Holy Spirit. His wisdom becomes our wisdom, His understanding becomes our understanding, and His thoughts, opinions, and moods become ours.

Early on in my ministry I was experiencing miracles in my life and received many kingdom observations, but I was still hungry for more. I was in a time of pressing in and seeking God to take me to another level. As I pursued Him, He spoke to me that I needed to grow in my relationship with Holy Spirit. I so loved praying in other tongues and functioning in a place of tuned-in living. I was in hot pursuit of deeper relationship. The Father began to reinforce to me the reality of Holy Spirit and His mind. He told me to interact with Him as I would a person. When I would receive little promptings or bits of information during times of ministry, He led me to acknowledge Holy Spirit in those moments, thanking Him, talking directly to Him, and acknowledging His role in the process. He also laid it on my heart to address Holy Spirit frequently. I began to call Him by name in my prayer time. I had known the presence of Holy Spirit and all of His fascinating functions, but the Father was opening up the revelation of the person of Holy Spirit to me. This directive fueled my level of downloads and observations.

HE IS YOUR TEACHER

Over and over in Scripture we see Holy Spirit presented as a helper to us. In fact, He is *the helper*. One of the primary ways that He helps us is serving as our own personal teacher. In John 14:26, Holy Spirit is identified as our teacher. He is brought onto the scene to educate us in the ways of the kingdom. Teaching is the act of giving lessons in order to enlighten a person on a particular subject. Simply put, we are the students, hungry to grow and advance; Holy Spirit is there with the lesson plan, vibrantly unfolding the ways of the kingdom to us.

Holy Spirit fills a stunning role as our personal teacher. Embracing His ministry unlocks exploits and empowers dreams. People often feel completely paralyzed and overwhelmed by God-sized revelation, but Holy Spirit is on the scene to teach, lead, and assist. Diving deep into the revelation of His function and mission equips us for spiritual success.

Even in the realm of prayer, we have to be taught:

> He was praying in a certain place, and when He ceased, one of His disciples said to Him, "Lord, teach us to pray, as John also taught his disciples."
> —LUKE 11:1

The disciples were inspired by the prayer life of Jesus. This is the verse before the Lord laid out what we call the Lord's

Prayer. They asked Him to teach them how to pray. This seems quite counterintuitive. After all, isn't prayer simply communication with God? Shouldn't it just be something that flows out of us? The short answer is yes, but there are layers and methods of prayer. There are effective and ineffective prayers. Prayer is like a currency or gateway that moves things from the heavenly realm to the earthly realm. Prayers in the earthly realm also influence and affect the heavenlies:

> Truly I say to you, whatever you bind on earth will be bound in heaven, and whatever you loose on earth will be loosed in heaven. Again I say to you, that if two of you agree on earth about anything they ask, it will be done for them by My Father who is in heaven. For where two or three are assembled in My name, there I am in their midst.
> —MATTHEW 18:18–20

Angels are dispatched by prayer. Demons are restricted by prayer. The highway in the space above our heads is regulated by decree. We have the ability to release things and bind things. We must learn how to operate in the place of governing prayer and declaration. This is not a skill that comes as a birthright, but one that is developed through revelation of position, identity, authority, and prophetic fluency. The more that we tap the mind of God, the more explosive and transformative our prayers become.

Holy Spirit is our language teacher. He is sent on the scene to teach us how to talk. He wants to fill our mouths with power and authority. Our mouths are gateways that unlock spiritual realms and promises. Depending on how we steward the gate, we will either walk in blessing or cursing. Our mouth is intended to release kingdom blessings and heavenly declarations. Our words are not supposed to give evil reports or agree with what hell is saying:

> Let no unwholesome word proceed out of your mouth, but only that which is good for building up, that it may give grace to the listeners. And do not grieve the Holy Spirit of God, in whom you are sealed for the day of redemption. Let all bitterness, wrath, anger, outbursts, and blasphemies, with all malice, be taken away from you. And be kind one to another, tenderhearted, forgiving one another, just as God in Christ also forgave you.
> —EPHESIANS 4:29–32

> Out of the same mouth proceed blessing and cursing. My brothers, these things ought not to be so.
> —JAMES 3:10

One of the primary things that grieves Holy Spirit is our words. When we speak the wrong things, it goes against the mind, attitude, and plans of Holy Spirit. He is standing at attention to teach us how to declare the will of God, the mind of God, and the plan of God. He teaches our tongues to function as prophetic instruments, releasing key words that open up doors.

Everything in the spirit realm is created by words. When we examine the story of Creation found in Genesis, we do not see God using His hands but rather His words. This is how the spirit realm functions. This is one of the power principles of the prophetic. We must release the word to receive the miracle! Our words are like containers; we fill them with faith or doubt, miracles or bondage, break-through or burden.

PROPHESY THE PROMISE

About four or five years ago I was in a time in my life of pressing deeper into my personal destiny. It seemed as though I was caught up in an ongoing prophetic explosion. Over and over the Lord would speak to me about the shift and the expansion of my steps. Many promises given to me in my personal prayer time were validated as others would speak the word over me.

Fortunately I understood how to follow the trail and see the prophetic bread crumbs. When there is major transition or elevation at hand, the Lord will inform you in a variety of ways, through several sources, on many occasions. It is vital to recognize that the promise is only the first step. Far too many people just plop down after receiving a word about their future; they mistakenly assume that they play no role in the fruition of that revelation. I can't say it enough: prophetic leading is always an invitation to prayer. You pray, and then you obey! This accelerates the prophetic process in your life.

As the Lord kept reassuring my heart about what was to come, I began to seek Him for instruction: "Lord, what do You want me to do? How should I pray?" The right declaration opens the right doors. Do not operate in a spirit of assumption thinking that you have the answer simply because the promise has been revealed. You need to know what to say. What should you prophesy to release the next level?

As I pursued, the word of the Lord came to me. The Lord told me to begin to thank Him daily that Joy and I walk under the ordination of heaven. He told me to make this a part of my continual prayer and thanksgiving. We want ordained plans, ordained doors, ordained steps, and ordained relationships with no delays, no hindering devils, and no deception. I went to town praying this every day, and it got down in my spirit and mind. The more you declare heavenly things, the more you become lifted into heavenly realms and removed from the beggarly elements of the natural world. My faith increased that my family and I would navigate divine plans.

Over the next couple of years I was tremendously blessed by the sudden release of kingdom relationships, the protection of the Lord relationally, and the opening of so many great doors. The shift that I heard, saw, and knew had come to pass. This was the fruit of my profession! Where did these words come from? My personal language teacher.

TOOLS FOR REVELATORY INCREASE

In embracing the role of Holy Spirit as teacher, there are tools for revelatory increase. One of those tools is meditation:

> Let the words of my mouth and the meditation of my heart be acceptable in Your sight, O LORD, my strength and my Redeemer.
> —PSALM 19:14

This verse in Psalms displays the powerful dance of words and quiet meditation. As our language teacher, Holy Spirit helps us know what to say and when to say it. He assists us in the known language and the unknown. He lovingly guides us down the pathway of development in the prophetic art of speaking.

He is also on call to assist us with the quiet inner conversation that is vital to unlock our understanding of the written Word. There is an inner rhythm that is key to releasing insight. We have to learn how to break down kingdom concepts and digest them so that we properly nourish our minds and spirits. Meditation is a critical part of that process. I am not talking about what so many false religions have named meditation; it is not twisting yourself into a knot and assuming a physical position. In fact, this process has little to do with your body and much to do with your mind and spirit. Meditation is the digestive system of the kingdom. It is during these quiet times of inner conversation and reflection that you break down God's wisdom into bite-sized nuggets.

Scripture even mandates meditation:

> Meditate on these things. Give yourself completely to them, that your progress may be known to everyone. Take heed to yourself and to the doctrine. Continue in them, for in doing this you will save both yourself and those who hear you.
> —1 TIMOTHY 4:15–16

According to the *KJV New Testament Greek Lexicon*, the Greek word here for *meditate* means "to devise, plan, practice, exercise myself in, study, and ponder."[2] Paul was advising Timothy to give attention to the Word by pondering (thinking deeply), studying diligently, and exercising. It is deeper than just a casual glance at a scripture or a typical reading. It is to engage both the spiritual and natural senses (mind, thought, and reason along with prayer, speaking, and pondering). This opens the gateway of your inner man to receive greater revelation. Stay in a particular chapter or verse of the Bible, praying and pondering until God speaks to you in some way about it. Paul was advising Timothy that a lifestyle of meditating on the Word of God would keep his belief system strong and avoid shipwreck.

Perhaps one of the most familiar and encouraging passages of Scripture that references meditation on the Word is found in Joshua:

> This Book of the Law must not depart from your mouth. Meditate on it day and night so that you may act carefully according to all that is written in it. For then you will make your way successful, and you will be wise. Have not I commanded you? Be strong and courageous. Do not be afraid or dismayed, for the LORD your God is with you wherever you go.
> —Joshua 1:8–9

The audacity of these verses is shocking. God is literally telling Joshua that he has the power to cause his steps to be blessed. Think on that. The power of blessing is in the hands of Joshua as he aligns with God's plan. What is the qualification for the blessing? Meditating on the promise! Joshua could plant himself in the blessing by planting himself in the Word. These promises hold just as true for you and me. We can unlock tremendous channels of supernatural breakthrough and favor by establishing ourselves deep in the Word of God and receiving heavenly downloads.

The Hebrew word here for *meditate* holds a slightly different meaning than the Greek word we examined earlier. According to the *KJV Old Testament Hebrew Lexicon*, this word means "to make a sound, to mutter, to moan, to muse, to ponder, to devise, and to declare."[3] Those are just some of the definitions associated with this particular word. In this instance meditation is a heart and mouth connection. It is speaking the Word and praying while pondering, and then repeating the cycle. There is a powerful access granted when the Word gets in your mind, your mouth, and your spirit!

When we are meditating on the Word of God, we are reflecting. We are searching to go deeper. During these times, we consciously tune in our spirit ears and eyes to the Lord for direction and clarity. As we sit in His presence, we open up the canvas of our heart for God to paint His truth upon. We pray, speak, and contemplate until God's voice is distinguished. We make a firm decision to be still on the inside, shutting down the noise, the distractions, and the mind traffic in order to focus in on His revelation. These times can be potent times of reset, when God takes us back to the starting point and erases the lies of the enemy. It is crucial that we engage in times of reflective seeking.

Another way we engage in seeking God for downloads is through quiet times of sitting in His presence. Just like meditating on the Word, we make an effort to shut down all the static in our minds and the busyness of our daily lives just to get calm in His presence. Scripture also mandates this approach:

> Be still and know that I am God; I will be exalted among the nations, I will be exalted in the earth.
> —PSALM 46:10

Notice that the verse here tells us to be still. Stillness is a choice. There are times that you just need to bask in the presence of God and open yourself up to hear His voice.

These can be tremendous seasons of dramatic spirit leading! Make that time to just be in His presence without striving.

Engaging Holy Spirit as teacher is absolutely critical for success as a child of God. It is virtually impossible to effectively pursue the kingdom and all of its glory without heavenly assistance. One of the most effective methods of help is insight and direction. As we learn to focus on Holy Spirit as our teacher, we become much more intentional about relating to Him as a person and making room for Him to unfold kingdom principles to us. Every pursuit has specific steps and actions. We can absolutely increase our level of guidance by applying these concepts and taking action.

#Prayer

I thank You, Father, for the downloads from heaven. Holy Spirit, we thank You that You are the great teacher, and we make room for Your lessons. I speak forth Your wisdom and insight to come into our lives. We do not tune You out, but we tune You in. You are speaking, and we are listening, in Jesus's name.

#Prophecy

I often find myself in seasons of prophetic preaching where I don't have a clue what the Lord wants me to say until I get a supernatural download! Many times I know He wants me to share from previous revelations and study, but other times He keeps me guessing! Sometimes He has told me to go to bed and trust Him to speak to me in the night. He challenges and develops my faith. As He was pouring out revelation to me, I asked Him, "Lord, what is this?" He said, "It is the download anointing, and it is for My prophetic voices in this hour."

He told me that there is grace for prophets and

prophetic people to receive revelatory messages and communication from heaven.

The real key is to tune in and listen. It's a grace (free gift). When you believe for it, it will come. You don't have to earn it to receive it. You lay claim to it by faith! In fact, I feel prompted to tell you to begin thanking the Lord for the download anointing! Get some verses about revelation and make it a part of your prayer time. Look for divine understanding.

There will be seasons of dramatic downloads—when the revelatory realm is so tangible. Then there are seasons where you walk out and live in what He has spoken. Don't get discouraged when there are not as many dramatic downloads. These things will come rolling in like waves. I saw sets of revelatory waves and breaks in between. Thank God for His downloads! We have full access to *all* the wisdom of God and the spirit of revelation.

Ephesians 1:17 says, "So that the God of our Lord Jesus Christ, the Father of glory, may give you the Spirit of wisdom and revelation in the knowledge of Him."

#Activation

Find one verse of Scripture and practice meditating on it. Read it, speak it, pray in the Spirit, and then ponder. Continue doing this during quiet time until you receive some type of insight. This will develop your skills in meditating on the Word of God and allowing Holy Spirit to teach you the Word.

#Downloads #Meditation #Insight

CHAPTER 5

THE POWER OF
SPIRIT PRAYING

. . . .

The Perspective of Heaven

EAVENLY DOWNLOADS ARE glimpses into the mind,
wisdom, understanding, and heart of God. In a single
moment the full understanding of God in a situation
is unfolded. Over and over again in my life this has been the
foundation for breakthrough and change.

I remember a dramatic experience a number of years ago
when a sudden download shifted the course of my life forever. I had recently planted a church and was hungry to grow
as a leader, so I took my team and attended a leadership
conference. The group hosting the event had a strong apostolic mandate for the nations. They planted churches all over
the world and burned to see souls come into the kingdom
of God. In one session they cast vision for the nations and
reaching the world. This subject pricked my heart in a dramatic way because it is a huge part of my mandate.

At age seventeen I had an intense encounter with the
Lord in which He unfolded both my calling and my commission. He explained to me that each person has both a

calling (their primary office or purpose) and a commission. The commission is how you will fulfill the call on your life. The Lord showed it to me by explaining that you can line up five pastors; they all hold the same office but have different commissions. Each pastor may fulfill their office with a different emphasis and mission. He told me about my office, and then He told me that I was commissioned to the nations to demonstrate His power. This has been a driving force at each unexpected turn and each new assignment in my life. I'm always looking for the proper way to be not only a proclaimer, but also a demonstrator.

A few years later, when I was leading a Bible college, I had another encounter that knocked me out of my chair in my office! I wept as the Lord reminded me of His purpose for nations in my life. Since then the mandate has increased and has even had extended times of major assignments within my beloved nation of America.

With this background, it was no surprise that during the leadership conference I was attending, as they began praying for people to be sent to nations, I heard the Lord tell me to embark on a global tour. "How would this work?" I remember asking. I was still building a new church. With faith and daring obedience, we arranged all the details, and I set my course to preach in seven nations in three weeks. It was a whirlwind of fire and glory. I took a small team with me, and we saw such explosions of the power of God! There were such phenomenal miracles, people were saved and delivered, and the kingdom expanded during our apostolic journey. One of the nations that I visited was Croatia. It was there that an unusual miracle took place. We were meeting in a theater that was so crowded with people that it was standing room only. The Lord began to release His anointing for miracles. A young lady was standing near the front with a terrible skin affliction. Jesus poured new skin over her that night, and no person was touching her. The pastor of the church witnessed this miracle and afterward shared with me what had taken place. There was an unprecedented eruption of power in those meetings!

It was obvious that the Lord was opening that nation for me to return and minister. The following year we rented the convention center in the capital city and held a miracle and salvation outreach there. People came from all over the surrounding nations. We saw the largest salvation gatherings in the region as God confirmed His word with signs, wonders, and dramatic miracles.

During my time there I spent much time alone in my room praying in the Spirit and opening myself up to the mind of God. It was during a time of intimate prayer that a download shot through my spirit and the Lord told me, "Get down on your knees." As I bowed in His presence, He began to mantle me for that nation. I literally felt Him covering me in a garment of glory. He told me that there was a great assignment for me in that nation and told me that I would go back every year until He released me.

I kept returning, and each year we saw a major influx of souls along with mind-boggling miracles. I remember on one trip the hospital called to confirm a dramatic case of deafness being healed. I remember another time when we witnessed a whole group of deaf people suddenly began to hear as we prayed for them! It was an extraordinary time of miracles. There were also times of dramatic deliverances. One night a young man fell to his knees in front of me. I discerned darkness upon him and began to take authority over the powers of hell. He started pounding his fists in anger on the platform. The more he pounded, the harder I prayed! I persisted until the power of God hit him and God's delivering power set him totally free. I later found out that he had been involved in drugs and caused a tremendous amount of trouble in the youth ministry. After his deliverance he was no longer bound to drugs and became a great help to the church and the youth ministry. God is in the transformation business!

The heavenly download about Croatia shifted my personal course, but it also ignited a fire in the nation and affected my family. Through my journeys there I later connected with apostolic leaders from America who pushed my life and ministry forth. I would never have connected to those people were it not for that download. Downloads hold keys. When you hear from heaven, you are handed heavenly keys to unlock assignments and purposes. Croatia has played a special role in my life on several levels, but it all began with a series of downloads. My mom was single for years and determined that she would not marry unless it was supernatural. Guess what? God supernaturally sent her a man of God from Croatia! When God gives you a particular assignment, no matter how great or how small, you never know the multiple layers of blessing that are contained in it. Downloads unlock assignments, and assignments often unlock blessings. Get a download and be blessed.

PRAYING IN THE SPIRIT

There is perhaps no greater tool in the area of personal revelation and heavenly downloads than praying in the Spirit. When people determine in their own hearts to spend consistent time praying in other tongues, they are turning their minds, bodies, and hearts over to Holy Spirit to bring forth the very mind and understanding of heaven. Spirit Praying holds the potential to unlock realms of faith and mystery that have been seemingly locked in your life.

Spirit Praying is the great equalizer. Many people watch a powerful preacher who eloquently articulates the Word of God and they think, "I wish I could have insight like that, but I am just an average person." The reality is that when preachers preach, they are operating in a gift. God created them to declare His Word, and there is a special endowment of divine power flowing through them that is mesmerizing. The principles they are communicating are not locked away from the believer; they are reserved for us to discover!

Praying in tongues levels the field and puts every believer on a course of discovery. The mind of God is opened up and made clear as you pray in the Spirit. The great healing revivalist John G. Lake stated, "I want to talk with the utmost frankness and say to you, that tongues have been the making of my ministry. It is that peculiar communication with God when God reveals to my soul the truth I utter to you day by day in the ministry. Many times, I climb out of bed, take my pencil and pad, and jot down the beautiful things of God, the wonderful things of God that He talks out in my spirit and reveals to my heart."[1]

Praying in other tongues (unknown languages) is one of the functions of the diversities of tongues listed in the Book of 1 Corinthians:

> To one is given by the Spirit the word of wisdom, to another the word of knowledge by the same Spirit, to another faith by the same Spirit, to another gifts of healings by the same Spirit, to another the working of

miracles, to another prophecy, to another discerning
of spirits, to another various kinds of tongues, and to
another the interpretation of tongues.

—1 CORINTHIANS 12:8–10

This is the only gift in the family of these nine varied spiritual gifts that is multifaceted. There are various languages
available when a believer receives the baptism of the Holy
Spirit. Each language opens up a different channel of mysteries to the believer. This realm releases dimensions of the
power of God and propels a person forward in the assignment and revelation of heaven.

PURPOSE OF SPIRIT PRAYING

Within the multifaceted operation of other tongues there
are essentially four dominant flows:

1. Tongues for personal edification

This is the personal prayer language that is provided to
each believer to build them up.

But you, beloved, build yourselves up in your most
holy faith. Pray in the Holy Spirit.

—JUDE 20

This is the realm of tongues that creates personal growth
and momentum. It is the realm that bypasses human understanding and prays the perfect will of God every time.
Imagine always praying in concert with heaven's agenda.
That is what happens when we pray in the Spirit. This is an
unknown language that is given to us to access the wisdom
and authority of heaven. We are able to move in and out of
this type of prayer whenever we want to. Each moment that

we spend in prayer for personal edification releases strength and revelation.

2. Tongues as intercessional groaning

This is a unique expression of Spirit Praying that I call supernatural intercession. All of a sudden, heaven asks for the use of your voice and body to pray so deeply that there are unearthly groans and unusual sounds coming forth. This is standing in the gap between the plans of the enemy and a person, people, or a situation. This is supernatural and comes and goes as the Spirit wills, not as you or I will. We are simply available.

> Likewise, the Spirit helps us in our weaknesses, for we do not know what to pray for as we ought, but the Spirit Himself intercedes for us with groanings too deep for words.
>
> —ROMANS 8:26

3. Tongues for interpretation

This is an operation of an unknown language for the sake of a divine message for a person or people. In this manifestation a message is given in an unknown spiritual language and then the meaning of the message is given (interpreted) either by the same person or another person. This is a move of the Spirit as the Spirit wills, not as we will. When the message is given and properly interpreted, it is the equivalent of prophecy. This is a supernatural demonstration of God's mind to a person or people.

4. Tongues as a sign to the unbeliever

In the Upper Room, as the Spirit fell, many came from various places to see what in the world was going on. Had these people lost their minds? Why were they staggering, stumbling, and acting intoxicated? What was the meaning of the strange sounds going forth? These types of questions are still asked today.

> But God has chosen the foolish things of the world to confound the wise.
> —1 CORINTHIANS 1:27

Our natural minds cannot always comprehend when another realm is manifesting here on planet Earth. Sure, we can study the Bible and gain insight, but at some point we recognize that the ways of God challenge our human thinking. That was what was taking place at Pentecost. People were being confounded and could not figure out what was happening. In the midst of that move, something astounding happened!

> When this sound occurred, the crowd came together and were confounded, because each man heard them speaking in his own language. They were all amazed and marveled, saying to each other, "Are not all these who are speaking Galileans? How is it that we hear, each in our own native language? Parthians, Medes and Elamites, residents of Mesopotamia, Judea and Cappadocia, Pontus and Asia, Phrygia and Pamphylia, Egypt and the regions of Libya near Cyrene, and visitors from Rome, both Jews and proselytes, Cretans and Arabs—we hear them speaking in our own languages the mighty works of God."
> —ACTS 2:6–11

There was a sign happening in the midst of the outpouring. God was testifying to people through a unique operation of the gift of tongues—tongues as a sign to the unbeliever. He was witnessing through the lips of people who did not know the language they were speaking! They were speaking supernaturally by the Spirit with the intent to reach the hearts of man. This particular operation of tongues is when a person speaks a known language in the earth that their natural mind does not know. They speak it as a message by the Spirit. It is a soul-winning tool that comes and goes supernaturally as the Spirit wills.

PERSONAL EDIFICATION

The most common realm of tongues in our daily lives is tongues for personal edification, or as I like to call it, Spirit Praying. This type of praying forms a rich foundation for revelation to unfold in our lives. Spirit Praying is one of the primary prophetic engines in the life of a believer. If every Christian who is filled with Holy Spirit would give themselves over to Spirit Praying, there would be a rush of revelation and a dramatic move of God as we came into the maximum level of understanding the mysteries of God.

Let's talk a bit about the process of Spirit Praying. You must understand that the prayer is initiated in your inner man and not in your mind. This is a bit of a challenge for many of us because we are so used to functioning in the realm of reason and thought, but this language and experience comes from the realm of spirit and faith. When you pray in the Spirit, you are praying the mysteries of heaven out and building yourself up. It is like releasing building blocks and methodically stacking them one on top of another. If you continue long enough, you will eventually have a full-scale building!

HOLY SPIRIT AS YOUR PARTNER

Imagine what your life would look like if you partnered with Holy Spirit and together built a fortress of faith that the power of the enemy could not penetrate. This is available as you pray without fail in the Spirit. Spirit Praying *builds faith*.

One of your first obstacles to this is your own limited understanding. As you pray in the Spirit, your mind will try to resume control and you will often find your thoughts running way ahead. You may even feel dry and as though nothing is breaking, but that is not the case. Remember, when you pray in the Spirit, you are not involving your mental reasoning capabilities. This is why your mind quickly grows restless. It is not needed in this realm of prayer. You can play worship music or ponder certain things to occupy your mind, but your mind is not in charge of this process. However, your mind may very well be greatly involved in the impending download!

Spirit Praying unravels spiritual mysteries.

> For he who speaks in an unknown tongue does not speak to men, but to God. For no one understands him, although in the spirit, he speaks mysteries.
> —1 CORINTHIANS 14:2

The kingdom of God is as a mystery to those who live and move in the natural realm with no spiritual understanding. According to *Webster's*, the word *mystery* means "profound, inexplicable, or secretive quality or character," or "something not understood or beyond understanding."[2] Heavenly perspective is outside the realm of human rationale:

> For those who live according to the flesh set their minds on the things of the flesh, but those who live according to the Spirit, the things of the Spirit. To be carnally minded is death, but to be spiritually minded is life and peace, for the carnal mind is hostile toward God, for it is not subject to the law of God, nor indeed can it be.
>
> —ROMANS 8:5–7

Your natural mind is at war with the infinite wisdom of heaven. When you pray in tongues, you depart from the realm of fleshly deduction and soar into the realm of unlimited wisdom. You are no longer bound within the limits of what you know or do not know. You are released from your own thinking, your own logic, and your own conflicted thought process.

It is absolutely imperative that we understand that God has not stored up His mysteries to be kept hidden from us, but through our complete redemption, freedom, and new nature we have all access into the multifaceted mind of God. The mysteries are ours to discover! God actually invites us into His heart and mind to reveal Himself to us in a way that propels us upward in both understanding and living.

Spirit Praying is the track upon which we travel deeper into the mysteries. This is a vital concept that must be properly understood to receive the downloads heaven has for you. As you pray in tongues for personal edification, you are praying out the mysteries bit by bit, and you will grow in faith.

Why is this important? It is quite simple: without faith you cannot please God (Heb. 11:6). Faith is pleasing to God. Faith is the substance of that which you hope for, and it is also your evidence that it has been promised and provided

(Heb. 11:1). Think about a substance. That is a far different concept than an intangible thing floating somewhere out there in space. No, a substance is an actual thing that you can touch and feel. Faith provides structure to your belief. Faith brings it out of the realm of possibility and into the realm of reality. Faith is also the evidence. What exactly is evidence? It is proof of something. Without evidence it is difficult to say if a thing exists. When there is evidence, it crosses the threshold from being an idea to being a reality. Faith is the evidence that something actually exists. It is that thing that pulls a promise out of the realm of the spirit and manifests the thing right here in the earthly realm.

Faith moves things into dimensions. Faith causes doors to open and others to close. Faith forbids demons and demands action. Faith refuses to allow a promise to be stolen. Faith is not demonstrated by a person who believes maybe, possibly, somehow, someday, something could happen. No, that is not faith! Faith is a precise conviction with a target. It knows what it believes and it is fully persuaded of the reality of that belief. In the eyes of faith, it is already done. Faith is never past tense; it is present and active! This is why Hebrews 11:1 says, "Now faith is." Notice it does not say *later* faith is. It does not say *maybe* faith is. It says *now* faith is! Faith is speaking, decreeing, and standing right now.

Faith is the result of revelation. When revelation is released, faith is established and the evidence of heaven is revealed. This causes extreme confidence and conviction to burst forth in the human heart. You move from hoping it happens to being absolutely convinced that it is done. Simply put, when God speaks, faith is released.

When we pray in the Spirit, we are partnering with Holy Spirit to unravel the mysteries and receive the insight. Many people fall under the weight of condemnation because they get stuck in methodology instead of results. It is like analyzing how a train travels to a destination versus how a car gets there. At the end of the day, the mode of transport is less relevant than the actual arrival. Tongues takes you to the destination. Some people think they have to pray an hour. Others start praying and ten minutes into it their minds are wandering off and they quit. Then the enemy makes war on them and begins to release accusation. He condemns them by saying, "You didn't pray long enough." Each moment you spend Spirit Praying is like a link on a chain. It does not matter if that chain is made at one continuous time or if you add links one at a time; either way you end up with the same chain.

The key thing is to expect revelation from Spirit Praying. How and when it comes are irrelevant. It could come as a sudden download in your car, it could come as a dream in the night, or it could come right there during the prayer time. The downloads will come if you just stay with it.

As the mysteries are revealed, you will find that God will illuminate the Word to you. Suddenly a scripture will spring forth with an understanding that you never had before. He will pray out both the problems and the answers in your life. As He reveals His Word to you, faith is established and you move onto another level. Faith comes through revelation. God speaks, and believing is established. Praying in the Spirit unlocks the realm of mysteries, and the voice of God illuminates His Word, establishing you in faith.

Spirit Praying builds a deep reservoir of abiding peace.

A life without peace is like living in a toxic wasteland. It is an awful place to be. In our journey with God we are going to face challenges, mountains, and valleys and enjoy stunning victories. There are seasons and storms, exploits and setbacks. One of the sustaining forces in our lives is the supernatural peace of God.

You can be in the midst of the most distressing trial and have an uncommon peace that gets you through it. There is a connection between Spirit Praying and peace:

> For with stammering lips and foreign tongue He will speak to this people, He who said to them, "This is the rest. Give rest to the weary," and, "This is repose," yet they would not listen.
> —ISAIAH 28:11–12

I believe that Isaiah was prophesying about the wells that would open to God's children when Holy Spirit came to indwell us. Through stammering lips, praying in tongues will build a strong reservoir of supernatural peace that sustains us and keeps us cemented in the plan of God.

Spirit Praying brings the master teacher on the scene.

> But the Counselor, the Holy Spirit, whom the Father will send in My name, will teach you everything and remind you of all that I told you.
> —JOHN 14:26

When you hang out with Holy Spirit by praying in other tongues, you are releasing the master teacher. Think on this for a moment. The Spirit of the Word is brought onto the scene to begin explaining secrets and mysteries to you. This is one of the real power points of a dynamic relationship with Holy Spirit—you are communing with the greatest teacher of all time. If there was a best-selling book on any topic that you needed desperately in your life, and you read that book, you would access a certain level of enlightenment. If you had a chance to sit down and talk one-on-one with the author as he explained the information in extreme detail, your experience and insight would go off the charts. This is the access that you have in Spirit Praying; it brings the master teacher on the scene.

Spirit Praying protects us from deception.

One of the missions of Holy Spirit is to lead us into complete truth. He is assigned as a guard against deception. I can still remember when I first came to the Lord and did not know the Bible well at all. I was so hungry, but my level of biblical knowledge was so low. How would I ever be able to tell the real from the false? When someone presented me with new concepts, a prophetic word, or a ministry gift, how could I know if it was right? At the time this was a valid concern. There were many times when I would just feel this deep uneasiness and then a peace about going in another direction. I learned to discern the leading of the Lord by listening to both the check (when something was wrong) and the peace (when it was right).

Later I recognized these leadings to be protective methodologies of Holy Spirit. He can provide a check or a grieving when something is out of place. I remember a time when I was given a particular teaching to listen to from a ministry friend of mine. I took this teaching and began listening to it in my car. I was only a few minutes into the message when I became so grieved that I could not continue listening. I grabbed that teaching tape and threw it away immediately. The man later asked me what I thought, so I told him. He challenged me and asked how I could know something was wrong when I didn't even listen to the whole thing. My reply was simple: I had a massive check. That is all I need to know that there is something wrong. As I prayed about the situation, the Lord revealed to me that the minister was camouflaging a life of deep immorality and that was the motive behind the false teaching. Many years later that all came out. I could have wasted valuable time and become entangled with wrong influences by not trusting my born-again spirit and the leading of Holy Spirit. I could have waited for my intellect to catch up with Holy Spirit's leading, but the reality is that we don't have time to waste. When we get a check, we need to listen and not allow the devil to rob us.

Spirit Praying builds a fortress of protection and creates an inner guard against deception.

> I have written these things to you concerning those who deceive you. But the anointing which you have received from Him remains in you, and you do not need anyone to teach you. For as the same anointing teaches you concerning all things, and is truth, and is no lie, and just as it has taught you, remain in Him.
> —1 JOHN 2:26–27

We have an anointing abiding in us for our protection. As we pray in other tongues, we are activating that guidance system and keeping ourselves on course. Holy Spirit will take us far beyond our own knowledge or insight and keep us planted in right thinking, believing, and living.

Spirit Praying releases inner rivers of refreshing, healing, strength, and glory.

We are not called to live in a dry place void of living waters and renewal. We are called to live in the rushing rivers of

Holy Spirit with all of His glory. Spirit Praying releases inner rivers of refreshing, healing, strength, and glory. There are multiple rivers available to you and me to empower us for supernatural living. So many believers attempt to walk out the supernatural through head knowledge, but it just will not work.

> On the last and greatest day of the feast, Jesus stood and cried out, "If anyone is thirsty, let him come to Me and drink. He who believes in Me, as the Scripture has said, out of his heart shall flow rivers of living water." By this He spoke of the Spirit, whom those who believe in Him would receive. For the Holy Spirit was not yet given, because Jesus was not yet glorified.
> —John 7:37–39

We must have the rivers of living water to break down the barriers and embark on exploits.

#Prayer

I pray for divine hunger for us. I ask for the release of mighty Holy Spirit rivers from deep within us. I call forth fresh wind, fresh fire, and living waters to flow. Lord, I thank You for a fresh infilling today and a power encounter with You, in Jesus's name.

#Prophecy

I have heard the Lord say, "I have transitioned you to a new place, a new realm…higher, deeper…moving in realms of fire, mantled (clothed) in a garment of fire….Speak with tongues of angels to nations…. Bring forth heaven's decree. These are prophetic times and demand prophetic utterances to bring the people forth."

#Activation

If you have received your prayer language and speak in other tongues, begin to challenge yourself to ramp up your time spent Spirit Praying. After you pray, tune in and expect downloads. They could come at any time and any place, so be on the lookout!

If you have never received your heavenly prayer language, pray this prayer out loud with your mouth: "Father, I ask You today to release the inner rivers of Holy Spirit. Fill me today to overflowing. I want to speak with new tongues! I want to pray out mysteries. I want the baptism of Holy Spirit and fire! Release Your fire now in Jesus's name!"

Now seek Him and spend some time in His presence. Play your favorite worship music, and let the sounds burst forth from your inner man. It may be a couple of sounds or full sentences—let it flow!

One of my family members prayed a prayer like that and did not speak in tongues instantly but began to speak in the middle of the night! When you pray and believe, you are filled. It is just a matter of shutting your intellect down and letting the spirit sounds come forth.

#SpiritPraying #PrayAndProphesy #NewRealms

CHAPTER 6

CREATE A PERSONAL PROPHETIC ATMOSPHERE

· · · · · · · · · · · · · · · · ·

Dealing with Fear

ATMOSPHERES ARE POWERFUL both individually and corporately. Faith creates an atmosphere that empowers promises; doubt creates a toxic atmosphere of defeat and lies.

To develop a lifestyle of revelation, you must be intentional about creating a prophetic atmosphere. In this chapter we will explore practical steps to create and maintain an atmosphere that hears from heaven.

I will never forget my intense battle with the spirit of fear. Early in my childhood I was exposed to this spirit as a result of what seemed like a harmless prank. The enemy created a situation where I was told spooky stories as a toddler while confined in a dark space. The enemy was sowing a seed that he intended to cultivate into lifelong bondage. This is how the power of darkness works. The wicked one sets us up for what he hopes will be enduring struggles. I have a tremendous amount of loathing for that foul spirit. The childhood encounter initiated an ongoing experience with the very tangible atmosphere and bondage of fear. This spirit of fear was not from God:

> For God has not given us the spirit of fear, but of power, and love, and self-control.
> —2 TIMOTHY 1:7

There is a dimension of fear that is beyond the realm of thought or emotion. There is an actual spirit of fear that attacks people, releasing intimidation, limitation, and panic. In my own life there was a well-coordinated series of attacks that created a long-lasting struggle with the spirit of fear. I was so deceived that I actually enjoyed fueling the spirit of fear. I watched scary movies, enjoyed ghost stories, and couldn't wait for the next "haunted house" attraction. All of these things only fueled the bondage. Demon spirits thrive in atmospheres of unbelief and false spiritual practices. Part of the work of bondage is to convince a person to build an atmosphere that creates a spiritual climate. I was so bound by the spirit of fear that I lived in a climate of fear itself. There were multiple supernatural encounters that only reinforced the ungodly work of fear.

After I got born again, everything shifted in my life. One of the defining moments was when I heard the voice of the Lord telling me to embark on a new adventure by going to Bible college. This decision made absolutely no natural sense, but it was a critical part of my redemption story. When I arrived at the school, I sensed a freedom and authority that I had never known. The atmosphere was charged with faith. The founder of the Bible college was a renowned faith teacher who regularly experienced tremendous miracles as a result of his authoritative stand on the Word of God.

Fear and faith are exact opposites. Faith is a heavenly building block. We believe by faith. We receive by faith. We live, move, and speak by faith. By faith we boldly and unwaveringly stand upon the promises of God. By faith we speak to mountains and command storms to cease. There is absolutely nothing that is impossible in the realm of faith! Jesus said, "If you can believe, all things are possible to him who believes" (Mark 9:23). There is no part of faith that accepts impossibility. Faith seizes upon the promise and extracts the potency of heaven. Faith unlocks the miracle realm and launches us into the arena of divine breakthrough.

Fear binds, hinders, and limits. In the demonic realm fear is the building block of unholy bondages. Fear causes a person to shrink back from his potential and the prophetic promises over his life. Fear causes a person to remain stuck, even though God is urging him onward. Fear is the foundation for the work of hell in the life of a person.

As I began to sit in the atmosphere at the Bible college I was attending, it was as though a hard shell of unbelief was being chipped away each day. What was the difference? Why was my deliverance springing forth after years of bondage? It was the power of the atmosphere. I was in a climate that was rich in faith, strong in authority, and bold in demonstration.

The atmosphere was created by preaching, teaching, praying, and design. The leadership had very intentionally planned and created an environment conducive to the fulfillment of the promise of God and the rich deliverance ministry of Jesus. As I received prayer, studied the Word, and soaked up the power of God that was present, I was completely set free from the spirit of fear. One atmosphere undid the creation of another atmosphere. The power of the kingdom overwhelmed the powers of darkness!

To walk in the supernatural and live in the realm of divine demonstration, we need to be very intentional about creating a personal prophetic atmosphere. It is one thing to attend a conference with a rich prophetic flow or to go to a church that values and moves in the prophetic. These atmospheres can be absolutely invaluable in your own spiritual growth and development. But if you are going to personally unlock the supernatural in your life, you must unlock the realm of revelation.

Many people make the tragic mistake of simply thinking that if God wants to speak to them, then He will. They are blasé in their pursuit of prophetic revelation. They place all the responsibility on God and fail to recognize the critical link between their diligence and hearing. The reality is that each of us can and will hear from God in such a way that supernatural breakthroughs and miracle encounters are unveiled.

ATMOSPHERES OF WORSHIP AND GLORY

When the builders laid the foundation of the temple of the LORD, the priests in their apparel stood with trumpets and, from the Levites, the sons of Asaph stood with cymbals to praise the LORD, following the example of David king of Israel. They sang responsively, praising and giving thanks unto the LORD, "For He is good, for His mercy endures forever toward Israel." And all the people responded with a great shout when they praised the LORD, because the foundation of the house of the LORD was laid. Now many of the older Levitical priests and chiefs of the fathers' households who had seen the first temple wept with a loud voice as the foundation of this temple was laid before their eyes, though many others shouted exuberantly for joy. As a result, the people could not distinguish the noise of the shout of joy from the noise of the weeping of the people since the people had raised such a loud noise that could be heard from afar off.

—Ezra 3:10–13

The people partnered with the vision of the Lord to build the temple. They were passionate about honoring the presence of God. You will always find that honor unlocks glory. When you honor and place esteem on what God is doing, you will open up realms of glory over your life. Atmospheres of honor are filled with glory and power.

As the people began to worship the Lord with total abandonment, His glory came in like a flood. There was a tidal wave of glory and rich movement of Holy Spirit. The sound began to increase; some were weeping while others were shouting. This is often one of the results of a revival atmosphere; Holy Spirit moves in such a way that different people have different reactions. Some are overtaken with laughter while others shake and tremble. Some people laugh as the joy of the Lord fills their mouths. Their struggle is replaced with the dew of heaven and victory overwhelms their souls. Of course this irritates and agitates the religious because they simply do not understand the move of the Spirit.

In these atmospheres of glory great wonders and miracles happen! I was traveling recently when the glory of God swept into the meeting where I was preaching. As we praised God, our praise unlocked the worship; as the worship came forth, the glory level began to swell like a rising tide. The Lord has taught me that there is a tide level of glory in corporate gatherings. When the level rises high, people get swept up. When people get swept up, miracles burst forth suddenly, like popcorn. I love the suddenlies of God! In a suddenly, impossible things happen. In a suddenly, oppression is broken. In a suddenly, the tide of depression is turned. In a suddenly, a financial miracle springs forth.

As I was ministering, I sensed the suddenlies of God coming. The Lord spoke to me about a person with a blind eye. He told me that it was only one eye that needed a creative miracle. He told me that if I would act upon His word, a miracle would come forth. One of the things that we must learn is to create and partner with atmospheres of glory.

I see the glory like a dense fog. When it comes rolling in, there is potential for any and all types of miracles. Obedience is the key that unlocks the miracle realm in glory atmospheres. To experience a miracle, you must be willing to believe bravely. What does that mean? It means to take uncommon risks. The miracle realm is risky; you have to lay it all on the line and say what Jesus is revealing to you.

I just shared what I sensed and saw. There was a tall lady in the very back of the room who responded and told me it was her. I love that Jesus knows everyone in a gathering. He is attentive to each need present. The glory will get the needs met. Many churches have people filled with needs, and they try to meet them all with programs, but they have no glory! They do not prioritize an atmosphere of glory. They do not sing songs about the glory. They do not preach about the glory. They really don't want the glory to show up because it will wreck all of their man-made plans.

As the lady with the blind eye came forth, I had a great reassurance from the Lord that she would be healed. The atmosphere of glory was rich. I prayed for her and nothing happened. She reported that she was no better. I prayed again. This is a vital key. We must not just respond to what we sense or feel; we must press in for the word of the Lord. Sometimes it takes a real tenacity to unlock what heaven says. God appreciates faith, and He honors it. Faith has no quitting sense. After the second prayer, she saw light, but no shape. This was an improvement from the first prayer. I went for it again and prayed another time. I then put my hand in front of her face and she suddenly grabbed it as she exclaimed, "I can see!" Jesus had opened her blind eye and released a powerful miracle!

SUPERCHARGED ENVIRONMENTS

What is an atmosphere? One of the definitions for the word *atmosphere*, according to *Webster's* dictionary, is "a surrounding influence or environment."[1] Atmospheres are environments; they are birthing places of experiences, thoughts, and feelings. You have physical, emotional, and spiritual responses to various atmospheres. I recall a recent trip that I made to Arizona with my wife. We were both amazed by how differently our bodies felt in the dry climate of the southwestern United States. My wife's skin responded totally differently to that environment than the moisture-rich humidity of the southeastern United States. The air felt different, and the temperature seemed less severe because of the lack of moisture. Both of our bodies responded completely differently to the variables in that region.

I recently visited one of the leading Christian media ministries in the world. I walked into the media center and could instantaneously sense the creative juices flowing. People were buzzing around, working on web projects, music projects, and video projects. The average staff member was wearing trendy clothes and looked creative. The place was alive with spark, flair, and energy. The least creative person in the world would be inspired there.

Have you ever visited any of the Disney theme parks? They have people on their creative staff called *imagineers*. They are tasked with designing and implementing environments that transport people in their imaginations away from the location of that park to "the happiest place on Earth." This is the ultimate expression of creativity. True creativity paints a picture that is so vivid, it feels real to the senses. People will pay hundreds, if not thousands, of dollars to experience that type of ambience.

In the realm of the spirit, words can be powerful catalysts for the creation of environments. When people raise their voices in their homes, screaming and cursing their children, and calling them all sorts of names because of the anger they are feeling in the moment, they give way to a spirit of anger and rage. The climate becomes toxic as strife fills the place. Not to say that on any given day a parent will not make a mistake. Each of us has had the experience of saying something we immediately knew was wrong. Holy Spirit quickly checks our heart and we know that we should not say and do such things, and we should not create such a toxic atmosphere. Thank God for His grace in these matters! We can very quickly come before the throne of grace and receive mercy: "If we confess our sins, He is faithful and just to forgive us our sins and cleanse us from all unrighteousness" (1 John 1:9).

What would happen if families were intentional in creating atmospheres of peace, love, and acceptance? I believe this would give birth to a different set of feelings, thoughts, ideas, and experiences. As priests and kings (Rev. 5:10), we have the responsibility to establish an atmosphere in our home that honors God. Entire families could be swept up into the majestic plans of heaven and receive tremendous healing if parents got radical about shifting the climate of their homes.

As supernatural people we must be diligent in creating right atmospheres. In Jesus's earthly ministry there was an intense environment of power and miracles. People sought Him out. They wanted to touch Him and receive the healing flow. Everywhere He traveled, there was a robust dimension of power and wonders. You simply could not get around Jesus without experiencing the kingdom in all of its weight, glory, and authority.

> Jesus went throughout all Galilee teaching in their synagogues, preaching the gospel of the kingdom, and healing all kinds of sickness and all sorts of diseases among the people.
> —MATTHEW 4:23

A personal prophetic atmosphere is a necessity for a believer who desires to live in kingdom power and authority. There is really no example of New Testament living that is powerless and void of the supernatural. This type of thinking is the result of humanism and religious politics. The gospel was preached and demonstrated with power. From the Old Testament to the New Testament, people experienced the kingdom of God in supernatural ways. God is not a set of principles or ideas. He is not a ten-step program or a self-help philosophy. He lives in the realm of glory. You cannot encounter God without experiencing heavenly things. Miracles and unexplainable phenomena should be commonplace for Christians.

Let's begin by establishing what the word *prophetic* points us to. If we are going to be focused on establishing a prophetic environment in our personal lives, we must bring definition to what that means. The latter part of the verse in Revelation 19:10 gives us good definition of the *prophetic*: "For the testimony of Jesus is the spirit of prophecy." Prophetic experiences, words, and revelation in their purest form reveal the heart and nature of Jesus. A prophetic climate is one that is designed to seek and find the person of Jesus. Anything less than that is hollow deception.

Creating a prophetic atmosphere begins by placing high value on the revelation of Jesus. You start at the foundation.

> He is "the stone you builders rejected, which has
> become the cornerstone."
> —ACTS 4:11

The cornerstone (or foundation stone) comes from the ancient building practice of masonry in which they laid a primary stone. All other stones would then be placed based upon the position of this first stone. In many ways this was the most important stone to be set because it would determine the position and structure of the entire building. The cornerstone is the foundation. No building is any stronger than its foundation. Jesus is the enduring foundation of the ages.

LIFESTYLES OF GLORY

To create a personal prophetic climate, you must hunger for it. Hunger is a gift. Hunger must be expressed by seeking.

I will bless the LORD who has given me counsel; my affections also instruct me in the night seasons. I have set the LORD always before me; because He is at my right hand, I will not be moved. Therefore my heart is glad, and my glory rejoices; my flesh also will rest in security. For You will not leave my soul in Sheol, nor will You suffer Your godly one to see corruption. You will make known to me the path of life; in Your presence is fullness of joy; at Your right hand there are pleasures for evermore.

—PSALM 16:7–11

Hunger creates a commitment to pursuit. The author of this psalm describes a lifestyle that values the presence, insight, and pursuit of the Lord. The reward is guidance, perseverance, deliverance, and revelation. There are many people who want the insight without the time spent seeking. Prophetic people are people with an intimate relationship with God. That is the basis for all prophetic encounters and wisdom.

Create a prayer and pursuit place in your home. Build an arsenal of worship sounds that bring you into the presence of God. Learn to seek Him with loud eruptive praise and to sit quietly before Him in reverence of His might and strength. If you set daily time to meet with God and create a place of meeting, the presence of the Lord will wait for you there.

Beyond that, allow your life to become a living tabernacle. What is a tabernacle? It is a building that houses the glory. What are you called to be? A living glory house, a breathing temple filled with God's presence. Prayer is not just something that you do during the set time. It is a lifestyle. You should live with an ear that is bent toward the heart of the Father and engage in an unending conversation. It is amazing how your life will turn in exciting new directions when you agree to be on alert at all times. God can speak to you whenever He wants. Take the limits off your prayer life. Certainly set times and places, but live tuned in.

Learn to value revelation. The prophetic spirit is the spirit of insight, hidden wisdom, and intimate knowledge. Prophetic people see what others do not see, they hear what others do not hear, and they know what others do not know. The hidden wisdom of God is an invaluable tool. In fact, I would dare say that it is absolutely impossible not to excel in purpose when you tap into the wisdom of God. If you went to meet with a great thinking leader, you would most likely place high value on that time. You would carry something to record the information that you received. This is part of the process of creating a personal prophetic atmosphere—you place value on heavenly insight. You listen and lean in. You write and record what is revealed. You live with a longing to be enlightened by the Father.

Prophetic experiences are like files from heaven being suddenly opened. The various methods of communication are like heavenly roadways. The file can travel to you through a dream or a vision. It can come to you by the still, small voice or an inner knowing. These tools are important and learning about these avenues is part of our prophetic development, but the real emphasis needs to be on content over experience.

Prophetic people value revelation. It is a law of the Spirit that what you bless will increase. Honor is the placement of value on something. People are willing to pay a high price for anything they deem valuable. You can have two paintings from the same period hung side by side and one may be worth a million dollars while the other is not worth a thing. What is the primary difference? The value that is placed upon the artist.

This is one reason that the Bible states that money is an indicator of value.

> For where your treasure is, there will your heart be also.
>
> —MATTHEW 6:21

I was recently talking with a lady whose daughter suddenly became violently ill and doctors could not seem to help her. The family had no revelation of supernatural healing, so the attack continued. They heard of a highly acclaimed medical clinic with a great track record in dealing with similar cases. Guess what? They traveled several times to another state and paid large sums of money to get help. Why? They valued the ability of the clinic and the wellness of their daughter.

I am convinced that my life is on the pathway it is today because my family and I gave up everything to pursue the call of God. Our destiny was worth any price. Our wholeness was worth the cost. When you honor something, you bestow extravagant gifts upon it.

I meet people all the time who want to develop the prophetic spirit in their life, but they refuse to buy a book or attend a class. Some say that they just don't agree with paying for these types of things. This is such religious thinking! If you buy a book for ten to fifteen dollars and get a spiritual impartation plus a lifetime's worth of knowledge, it is well worth the investment. I recall a number of years ago I led two Bible colleges back-to-back. One was the school I graduated from. I had the time of my life leading those students; it is still one of my favorite life seasons. That school required students to pay tuition. The next school that I led had no tuition but received love offerings. The difference was drastic. The school with no tuition had a strong spirit of revival, but the students greatly lacked commitment. What was the problem? They did not value what had no price, and transformation has a price. There is a process of moving from point A to point B. It is the same with revelation. You must honor it, value it, seek it, and maximize it.

Another invaluable key to creating a personal prophetic climate is to become intimately acquainted with the person of Holy Spirit. You must learn to relate to Holy Spirit not as an idea but as a person, recognizing that He has methods, thoughts, ideas, and opinions. Holy Spirit can be pleased, and when He is, you will sense His attitude of approval over your life and actions. Holy Spirit can be grieved, and when He is, you will sense His displeasure in what was said or done.

As long as your relationship with Holy Spirit remains mystical and not practical, you will miss vital dimensions of the prophetic realm. You must study the scriptures regarding Holy Spirit and His ways. Read glory stories and learn of His moves. Talk to Him as a person and wait for the whispers of His voice. As you concentrate on Him, your vision in the spirit will clarify. You will learn to distinguish His ways and ideas.

For me, as I mentioned a few chapters ago, this began with the instruction from the Lord to interact with Holy Spirit on a more regular basis. I began to talk to Him and then wait for the inner conversation to unfold. I tuned in and acted on what I heard by faith. I stopped going into prayer without something to write or record. I prioritized hearing and acting on His promptings. Sometimes I missed it, but why focus on the times that you miss it when there are exhilarating times of supernatural results? That is what I choose to focus on. I begin most days by telling Holy Spirit, "Good morning." I lean on Him for wisdom throughout my day and in every place. This master key will kick-start your life of revelation! Talk to Him, listen to Him, wait on Him, and be quick to obey Him.

BECOME A CLIMATE SHIFTER

A prophetic atmosphere is presence based. Learn to fill your place of prayer with worship. Find music, sounds, and videos that unlock the presence of God in you. Play these sounds in your home and lift your voice in worship to the Lord. There are times to sit in silence or quiet reflection, but there are lots of times that we need to be loud and vocal in our adoration of our God. Far too many people are sitting when they need to be pursuing. Ask the Lord for His presence and learn to rest in that presence. Learn to soak in His presence. Learn to live in His presence. Prophetic people are presence people!

We are called to be climate shifters. Jesus did not go into regions and reflect the spiritual atmosphere. He shifted it with kingdom authority. Jesus set the tone; He shifted the atmosphere and released the kingdom. This is what kingdom people do!

> When Jesus finished these sayings, the people were astonished at His teaching, for He taught them as one having authority, and not as the scribes.
> —MATTHEW 7:28–29

If an atmosphere is created and maintained long-term, it will birth a climate. Climates give way to systems of thought (strongholds). Climates of extreme poverty produce generational mind-sets of lack and fear. Climates of radical faith create wild kingdom imaginations and dreams, where miracles are common and abundance is embraced. God is asking His people to create prophetic atmospheres and give birth to miraculous and sustained climates of revival!

#Prayer

I call forth a prophetic atmosphere in our homes. I pray we have eyes that see and ears that hear. Lord, I thank You for hunger that unlocks uncommon realms of seeking. As we seek You, Lord, I pray we find You in an amazing way in this season. I thank You, Lord, that You reveal when to pray, where to pray, and how to pray, in Jesus's name.

#Prophecy

This is a new level for you...Go without any fear or hesitation. Tap into the mind of the Spirit: unlimited revelation, direction, insight. No holdbacks! When the mind of the Spirit is unlocked, you have access to all the wisdom of heaven. You know how to do things, when to do them, where to do them...no limits. Every limit is removed by the revelation that comes through the mind of the Spirit. Minstrels' ministry help unlock that function, as does deep worship, intercession, giving birth to revelation, and sitting under the fountain of glory...as you would sit under a water fountain.

#Activation

Find a song that brings you into a place of worship and play that in your private place. Now sit before the Lord, waiting on Him for a thought, impression, or picture, and write what you see. Ask the Lord for a personal prophetic interpretation and instruction. No matter how simple it is, maximize it! Remain in the place of prayer until something is revealed to you. Prayer is a dialogue, not a monologue. You seek and you listen.

#ChroniclesOfRevelation #PenOfAReadyWriter

CHAPTER 7

EXPOSE THE LIES OF THE ENEMY

. . . .

Surrender Is the Key to Power

PERHAPS ONE OF the greatest blockages to functioning in revelation is the bombardment of the enemy against our own human minds. The devil understands just how powerful a thing it is to move in heavenly downloads. Once you have access to the mind of the Spirit, you also flow and function in the power of the Spirit. This was one of the key secrets of Jesus's earthly ministry. I believe that Jesus lived an uncommon life of radical obedience. His quest was to be dead center in the will of His Father at all times. There are few who live so daringly, so surrendered, but when they do, they walk in extraordinary power.

What would it look like if we too lived our lives in a place of complete surrender? We would not just be a generation who told people about Jesus, but we would demonstrate the power of God in our daily lives. This is the result of a life established in obedience. There is no shortage of power. The power of God flows freely like a river as we walk out the plans and purposes of our Father. Read what Exodus says about the Lord's power:

> Your right hand, O LORD, is glorious in power. Your right hand, O LORD, shatters the enemy.
> —EXODUS 15:6

God's power shatters the works of hell. If a generation functioned in the power of God, what would it look like? Bondages would be broken, minds renewed, lives forever changed, and the kingdom advanced. So many of God's children sit as beggars outside the gates of authority, wishing, hoping, and longing for His power, yet it is freely given to them. Lives planted in heavenly wisdom and revelation manifest kingdom power. Kingdom power crushes the works of hell!

> In the evening, when the sun had set, they brought to Him all who were sick and those who were possessed with demons. The whole city was gathered at the door, and He healed many who were sick with various diseases and cast out many demons. And He did not let the demons speak, because they knew Him.
> —MARK 1:32–34

The whole city was affected by the ministry of Jesus. What were they affected by? Was it His profound wisdom, His unique oratory skills, or His sense of humor? No. The thing that impacted the city the most was the movement of the supernatural power of God in their midst. This was an uncommon element. They were used to the religious elites who would come and give flowery speeches and renditions of the law without anything supernatural happening. As we look at much of the church world today, we can see the same phenomena. There are many great preachers who can deliver a sermon with unique skill and who possess a rich vocabulary, yet there is something lacking. The bound still leave bound, the sick have no access to healing power, and the church, as a whole, still lacks direction because there is no prophetic insight.

We are a people created for the supernatural. It is in our DNA. There is a longing inside us to connect with the Creator, and He is not a natural being. We are hungry to taste, touch, and experience the heavenly realm. Jesus came ministering in power and authority. He invaded the dark places with the light and power of God; sickness was crushed under the weight of the kingdom. The most difficult diseases had to leave and terrible demonic bondages easily fell away from people. This was the King moving freely in the realm of the earth and bringing forth a heavenly invasion.

SURRENDERED AND SEEKING

This is the picture of what our lives on Earth should be. We should become living, breathing access points for the kingdom of God. If a person lacks direction, then the gifts of the Spirit are available to operate and speak to him or her prophetically. If people are bound with demonic power, then the ministry of deliverance is available to set them free. If there is a long-standing sickness or a seemingly impossible case, then the healing wells spring forth. As believers we are called not only to possess the kingdom but also to be possessed by the King. He directs our steps, planting us in purpose and moving through us as He sees fit. We become kingdom releasers—issuing forth the power, glory, and weight of heaven itself into this earthly realm.

Jesus lived this life, and He did it through surrendering and seeking. He knew that His assignment was to destroy the works of hell:

> Whoever practices sin is of the devil, for the devil has been sinning from the beginning. For this purpose the Son of God was revealed, that He might destroy the works of the devil.
>
> —1 JOHN 3:8

Jesus's very existence was designed to crush the power and reach of the enemy. He continually exercised His authority over the devil, setting people free everywhere he went:

> In the synagogue there was a man who had the spirit of an unclean demon. And he cried out with a loud voice, "Leave us alone! What have You to do with us, Jesus of Nazareth? Have You come to destroy us? I know who You are—the Holy One of God!" Jesus rebuked him, saying, "Be silent, and come out of him!" When the demon had thrown him down in their midst, he came out of him and did not hurt him. They were all amazed and said among themselves, "What a word this is! For with authority and power He commands the unclean spirits, and they come out." And His fame went out to every place in the surrounding countryside.
>
> —LUKE 4:33–37

Jesus dealt with the enemy with authority. He did not give the devil a choice. He commanded Satan's power to be broken and cast him out. The religious people were totally stunned by this! They could not figure it out because they preached a powerless gospel of rules and regulations, completely void of manifestation or demonstration. The real gospel of Jesus brings healing, deliverance, and salvation.

I believe that one of the critical secrets to the level of power that Jesus walked in was His total surrender to God's will. Read what Jesus said:

> For I came down from heaven, not to do My own will, but the will of Him who sent Me.
>
> —JOHN 6:38

Jesus understood that a life of obedience was also a life of power. He lived from a place of total surrender. He delighted in the Father, and the Father delighted in Him.

The road of obedience was one of love. It was not one of constant toil; sometimes the will of God is challenging because our flesh wants to act crazy, but there is delight in the will of God. The will of God unlocks the favor of God; the will of God unlocks the miracles of God; and the will of God unlocks the blessing of God!

> Jesus answered him, "If a man loves Me, he will keep My word. My Father will love him, and We will come to him, and make Our home with him. He who does not love Me does not keep My words. The word which you hear is not Mine, but the Father's who sent Me."
>
> —JOHN 14:23–24

Jesus not only lived surrendered, He lived seeking. He had a deep well of prayer, which is another secret of the power of God. We must build wells of prayer in our lives. Simply put, prayer is communication with the Father. Jesus's foundation was prayer, and He went to the Father for instruction and guidance. He didn't move without heavenly instruction, and He sought it often:

> Yet even more so His fame went everywhere. And great crowds came together to hear and to be healed by Him of their infirmities. But He withdrew to the wilderness and prayed.
> —LUKE 5:15–16

I just love this picture of Jesus. In the midst of a time of great outpouring and multitudes coming to receive, He withdrew. He got alone. Why? Because He wanted to spend time with the Father. This is a powerful picture of what our prayer lives should look like. It should be much more of a divine romance than a drudgery of commitment. We should long for the presence of God, and our prayer lives are meant to be an expression of that hunger and love for the Father. I love how the author of this psalm paints such a vivid picture:

> How lovely is Your dwelling place, O LORD of Hosts!
> My soul longs, yes, even faints for the courts of the LORD; my heart and my body cry out for the living God.
> —PSALM 84:1–2

This is a cry of passion! This is not the writing of someone who dutifully goes into the place of prayer to recite a mechanical litany. This conveys the heart of a person whose very identity and breath are tied into the existence of the Almighty. Prayer is intended to be our life's breath. Prayer should be the canvas of our hearts upon which God's great masterpiece of inspiration is painted. Prayer is the place of quiet reflection, intimate longing, deep groanings, and mighty roaring. In the place of prayer, the rumble of revival comes forth as we cry out to the Lord for His kingdom.

A Love Relationship With Our Father

The concept of heavenly downloads and the idea of receiving communication from God should be completely normal in the life of a believer. In spite of the fact that we have been fully redeemed, the enemy seems to be successful at convincing us we cannot receive revelation from heaven. One of his key lies begins by communicating a false narrative of our Father. In order to fully enjoy the love relationship we are destined to have with God, we must cement two truths in our understanding of who God is and how He relates to us. The first truth is the reality that when we have been born again, we are children of God! We are no longer outside the covenant looking in; we are in the family of God. He is not relating to us as His slaves but as His kids.

> Giving thanks to the Father, who has enabled us to be partakers in the inheritance of the saints in light. He has delivered us from the power of darkness and has transferred us into the kingdom of His dear Son, in whom we have redemption through His blood, the forgiveness of sins.
>
> He is the image of the invisible God and the first-born of every creature. For by Him all things were created that are in heaven and that are in earth, visible and invisible, whether they are thrones, or dominions, or principalities, or powers. All things were created by Him and for Him. He is before all things, and in Him all things hold together. He is the head of the body, the church. He is the beginning, the firstborn

from the dead, so that in all things He may have the preeminence. For it pleased the Father that in Him all fullness should dwell, and to reconcile all things to Himself by Him, having made peace through the blood of His cross, by Him, I say—whether they are things in earth, or things in heaven.

And you, who were formerly alienated and enemies in your mind by wicked works, yet now He has reconciled in the body of His flesh through death, to present you holy and blameless and above reproach in His sight, if you continue in the faith, grounded and settled, and are not removed from the hope of the gospel, which you have heard, and which was preached to every creature which is under heaven, and of which I, Paul, have become a servant.

—COLOSSIANS 1:12–23

As verse 12 says, we are to be partakers of a glorious inheritance. Who gains access to an inheritance? Family members get the inheritance. This speaks of the fullness of the redemption that Jesus paid for on our behalf. We were taken out of the kingdom of darkness and given complete and total access to the kingdom of light!

Jesus is the firstborn (Col. 1:15). There is only a firstborn if there is a family. The picture that is being painted here is that of a family. Jesus was the forerunner. He opened up the gate for a family to emerge. When we were born again, we were supernaturally snatched from the dominion of hell and placed under the dominion of heaven from a position of ruling and reigning. At one time we were strangers, but the blood of Jesus and our faith in the power of His blood has made us heavenly citizens.

> And because you are sons, God has sent forth into our hearts the Spirit of His Son, crying, "Abba, Father!" Therefore you are no longer a servant, but a son, and if a son, then an heir of God through Christ.
>
> —GALATIANS 4:6–7

The Bible tells us that Holy Spirit was sent to us as a helper (John 14:26). He brings divine help into every area of our lives as we learn how to build relationship with Him. In this passage we see one dimension of the ministry of Holy Spirit is to reveal the position of the Father to us and unfold our position in Him. We have literally been given divine assistance to discover all that we are and who we are in our new nature. We have the vibrant ministry and gifts of Holy Spirit working inside us, unfolding the majesty of the King and of the kingdom.

We have passed from a place of slavery, from fear, to acceptance as sons. The Father has literally invited us to sit at the table of encounter with Him and discover His glorious riches.

With the discovery of who we are, there also comes a repositioning:

> "For in Him we live and move and have our being." As some of your own poets have said, "We are His offspring."
>
> —ACTS 17:28

With this repositioning, we are no longer functioning outside Him—trying to get His attention and assistance. We are functioning in Him! We are functioning in victory. We are positioned in healing. We are established in truth.

Not only that, but we also are seated far above all the power of hell.

Now that we have established our position, we need to comprehend a second powerful truth: that God is good and His plans for us are good.

> For I know the plans that I have for you, says the LORD, plans for peace and not for evil, to give you a future and a hope.
> —JEREMIAH 29:11

As He is a good Father, God has good plans for us. He has not established evil plans of destruction. Those types of plans are conceived in the corridors of hell.

The voice of religion has often formed a toxic narrative about the nature of God in our own minds. We have been programmed to relate to God as an angry being looking to get even with us, when in fact He wants to relate to us as a loving Father:

> What man is there among you who, if his son asks for bread, will give him a stone? Or if he asks for a fish, will he give him a snake? If you then, being evil, know how to give good gifts to your children, how much more will your Father who is in heaven give good things to those who ask Him!
> —MATTHEW 7:9–11

Jesus was preaching about the nature of the Father, that He wants to give good gifts to His children. He makes a stunning comparison between His nature and the nature of natural parents. How many of us work and plan to be able to position our kids in a better place than where we started?

No good parent intentionally plans for the failure and defeat of his or her kids. No good parent breaks his or her kid's leg to teach him a lesson. Yet this is the picture that is often painted of the Father by religion. Miracles, breakthroughs, and wonders are the plans of a very good Father. Your lifetime should be a quest to discover the goodness of your Father and all of His treasures.

WORSHIP AS A SON WORSHIPS

I learned a very valuable lesson one time about the power of the Father's goodness. I was away ministering at a revival meeting in a church. They had also invited a guest worship leader to do the music, and we were staying at the same place. He shared with me how he had grown up in a culture that emphasized works and achievement far above relationship. He learned at an early age the value of serving God, but he always had an internal deficit.

As he grew up, he heard of a dynamic, revival-oriented ministry and felt drawn by Holy Spirit to attend their school of ministry. He moved to a part of America he had never lived in before to attend the school. As he sat in the classes, the teachers opened the Word of God and began to proclaim the nature of God in a way that he had never personally discovered. He was learning about God, the good Daddy! It melted his heart and brought him into a realm of total joy. His mind was delivered and his heart set free.

While we were ministering in the meetings, I heard him wake up in the morning and begin to cry out to God. This was something I heard many times traveling with various teams around the world, but there was something so contagious about this man's praise. He kept calling out to Daddy.

He would say: "I love You, Papa. You are a good Daddy." He was worshipping not as a servant but as a son. I would hear his laughter as the joy of the Lord overwhelmed him. His relationship with the Father challenged me. I found myself constantly talking to my Daddy after that trip. It opened up a new level of understanding about the love of God and His vast mercy for me.

I was ministering in a city once and praying for a person to receive a healing miracle. The individual was plagued with pain and infirmity in a particular area of his body. I was praying and releasing healing, yet there was no instant change. All of a sudden, it felt as though someone released a dam in my belly and the goodness of God began to break forth. I forgot about the person and just started worshipping my Daddy. I started proclaiming how good He is. I was being swept up in a tsunami of His love and goodness.

I started jumping up and down getting totally lost in His presence. Suddenly I remembered that I had been praying for a healing miracle. I opened my eyes and saw the person standing in front of me also totally captivated by the presence of God. He was free from all the pain and began to move and do things he could not previously do. God had done a miracle! What pathway did the power travel on? The revelation of His goodness. What would a generation that discovers the deep abiding goodness of God look like? That generation would have no problem believing for outrageous miracles, crazy breakthroughs, and radical awakenings. I say, "Lord, let us discover Your goodness!"

The Father corrects us when we get off course, but even His correction is for our good.

My son, do not despise the chastening of the LORD, nor be weary of His correction; for whom the LORD loves He corrects, even as a father the son in whom he delights.

—PROVERBS 3:11–12

Even in times of discipline He is merciful and full of compassion. He does not deal with His kids through wrath but through mercy and a strong desire to see our lives unfold into a living display of His will. The tender correction of the Lord aligns us with His plan.

Romans 5:8 says, "But God demonstrates His own love toward us, in that while we were yet sinners, Christ died for us." Jesus did not die for us when we were acting right. He did not go to the cross because our hearts were right or we were demonstrating any type of appreciation. No! His act of surrender was one of love for us. Love is sacrificial, not self-serving. Love does what is right and what is in the best interest of the other person involved, even when it hurts. Jesus committed the ultimate act of love by giving His very life for a people who were wayward, rebellious, and lacking gratitude.

It is the revelation of the love and goodness of God that leads men and women to repentance: "Do you despise the riches of His goodness, tolerance, and patience, not knowing that the goodness of God leads you to repentance?" (Rom. 2:4). It is when we discover the heart of God that we fully open up and trust Him with our lives. There is something so powerful about relating to God as our Father and being so in love with Him that it is an easy thing to hear His voice and obey Him. The obedience begins to flow from a place of trust and love for Him. The Father gets excited over His kids' advancement and blessing.

There is a psalm that speaks about the heart of God for us:

> Let them shout for joy and rejoice, who favor my vindication; and let them say continually, "The LORD be magnified, who delights in the prosperity of His servant."
> —PSALM 35:27, NASB

How many people actually get this verse and believe it? In this writing we see the heart of the Father God on full display. He is gleefully excited when we prosper and do well. This is the nature of a true Father, always wanting to bless His kids.

Another vivid picture of the Father is found in this passage:

> The LORD your God is in your midst, a Mighty One, who will save. He will rejoice over you with gladness, He will renew you with His love, He will rejoice over you with singing.
> —ZEPHANIAH 3:17

Imagine for a moment a father singing over a young child and delighting as she responds in joy. See the child raising her hands, desiring Daddy to pick her up as he is singing her favorite song. I think this passage paints such an intimate picture of delight as the Lord sings over us and watches us enjoying the sound of His voice.

When religion talks you into embracing a false narrative of who you are and what your relationship with God looks like rather than allowing you to worship as a child of the Father, it manages to destroy faith for heavenly downloads.

This is one of the real deceptions that we must shatter. We must come to know that we are sons and daughters, being radically loved by a good, good Father with plans of peace and prosperity for us. This does not mean that we will not walk a narrow road or that there will not be struggles, but what it does mean is that God's goodness is all around us even in times of refining or challenge. He rich love for us and genuine concern for our well-being is powerfully present in every facet of our lives.

The enemy works over time to condemn the children of God. He uses evil lies in an attempt to conceal the reality of our identity and position in God. His ultimate aim is to dislodge believers from the position of victory that was won at Calvary. Agreeing with the lies of the enemy creates blockage of critical insight. Revelation is our portion! Spirit leading is a norm for the people of God. Learning who we are empowers receiving revelation. We must tear away the lies that bring condemnation and confusion.

> There is therefore now no condemnation for those who are in Christ Jesus, who walk not according to the flesh, but according to the Spirit. For the law of the Spirit of life in Christ Jesus has set me free from the law of sin and death.
> —ROMANS 8:1–2

The word *condemnation* here in the Greek language means "a damnatory sentence."[1] Condemnation is the power of accusation and judgment. When Jesus went to the cross, He took every sin, every mistake, and every shame, and nailed them there so that you and I might be free. The enemy is a professional accuser. He releases evil sentences and proclamations to us that are contrary to the reality of our covenant with God. The problem is the condemnation; the answer is to embark on the walk of the Spirit. There is absolute and complete freedom in Jesus. Holy Spirit is on the scene to help us discover that glorious exemption.

Killing the lie of condemnation is critical to embracing God's downloads for your life. You cannot have faith to receive heavenly communication as long as you believe the lie.

COMMON LIES THAT NEED TO BE EXPOSED

The following are common lies concerning heavenly downloads.

You deserve condemnation.

Condemnation is a powerful tool in the enemy's workshop to bind and afflict the people of God. Thank God, we can discover our true identity and freedom.

You are not smart enough.

The enemy lobs bombs at people's minds, claiming they need to be smarter, as if it takes a PhD to hear from heaven. This is an absolute fabrication invented by hell to rob faith and empower fear. In the Book of Numbers, chapter twenty-two, the Lord literally spoke through a donkey. He had no challenge filling the mouth of a simple animal. How much more should we expect Him to fill our hearts, minds, and mouths with heavenly insight? Our learning abilities and our scholastic achievements have absolutely nothing to do with our ability to receive downloads.

I am the LORD your God, who brought you out of the
land of Egypt; open your mouth wide, and I will fill it.
—PSALM 81:10

You are not qualified.

This is one of the most common accusations that is
released in every area. The enemy uses this lie to shackle us
to the weight of our own ability instead of leaning heavily on
God. The miracle realm is the realm of deep reliance. As we
have already discovered, it was Jesus's total surrender and
obedience that opened Him up to Earth-shattering exploits.
There is one thing and one thing only that qualifies us as
sons and daughters, and that is the blood of Jesus. Do not
accept any lie that takes you away from the blood. The blood
is where your redemption is. The blood brings you strength
and power.

> But Christ, when He came as a High Priest of the good
> things to come, by a greater and more perfect taber-
> nacle, not made with hands, that is to say, not of this
> creation, neither by the blood of goats and calves, but
> by His own blood, He entered the Most Holy Place
> once for all, having obtained eternal redemption.
> For if the blood of bulls and goats, and the ashes of
> a heifer, sprinkling the unclean, sanctifies so that the
> flesh is purified, how much more shall the blood of
> Christ, who through the eternal Spirit offered Himself
> without blemish to God, cleanse your conscience from
> dead works to serve the living God?
> —HEBREWS 9:11–14

It is just your imagination.

This is one of the common hindrances to hearing and
receiving the voice of God. You will often think it is just

your mind playing tricks on you. Now think about this for a moment: Why is it easier to believe in your ability to be deceived than in your ability to hear from heaven? This is just a religious lie. You have to stand firm in the promise in Romans chapter eight, that you are led by the Spirit of God (v. 15) and you are operating in the strength of His voice.

Your past is too ugly.

The enemy cannot point to the future because it spells defeat to him. He is so skilled at reminding you of the past, but the Bible tells us plainly that you are forgiven. You are in Christ and old things have passed away (2 Cor. 5:17). When God looks at you, He does not view you through the lens of your past. That accusation is a complete and total lie! You stand under the blood of Jesus Christ totally free and accepted by God.

Downloads are only for prophets.

It is true that the office of the prophet holds an uncommon mantle of revelation that speaks on a level that is profound, but being led by the Spirit is for all believers. This includes you and me! This means that you do not have to be a prophet to hear from God. In fact the church is told to seek the gift of prophecy.

> Therefore, brothers, eagerly desire to prophesy, and do not forbid speaking in tongues.
> —1 CORINTHIANS 14:39

This was written to God's people, not exclusively to prophets. We are all to seek the simple gift of prophecy to build each other up.

We don't need to get spooky.

This is a real cornerstone of religious thinking. There are all kinds of cute little sayings about being too spiritual or too heavenly minded: "Some people are just foolish." Or "It has nothing to do with God." I get what people are saying, but it is actually not too spiritual. It is just simply being goofy! Jesus was completely heavenly minded, yet He sure did a lot of earthly good. I think most people could use a little more heavenly minded activity in their daily lives. When we really hear from God and are mature in the things of the spirit, there is great fruit. Many of the bad experiences we have had come from deceived people operating either in a false spirit or a very carnal spirit. They blame their goofiness on God when it was just their own flesh. Why begin with a negative? This lie is as if going after God full bore needs some type of disclaimer. No, when you pursue and find God and His voice, you will actually become stronger and more solid.

You can only hear from God sometimes.

This is not true either. Romans chapter eight does not qualify itself that we are only led by the Lord on certain occasions. This is an excuse for spiritual apathy, and we must crush it. The reality is that spirit leading is a daily thing, but it comes in different ways, as we will discuss later. There are also times when we don't have as vibrant an experience or we do not need a new instruction because we are still on assignment from the last one.

Eye hath not seen...

This is a scripture that has been masterfully twisted and improperly preached by many.

But as it is written, "Eye has not seen, nor ear heard, nor has it entered into the heart of man the things which God has prepared for those who love Him." But God has revealed them to us by His Spirit. For the Spirit searches all things, yes, the deep things of God.

—1 CORINTHIANS 2:9–10

Religious preachers have shared the first part of this passage as a way of explaining that we will just never understand God. They have justified their own lack of faith and understanding by twisting these verses. They simply cannot comprehend living in line with the Bible or traveling a narrow path. Yes, God's ways are a great mystery to the world. There are things about God and His kingdom that are far beyond our natural thinking or understanding, but the reality is that God is not hiding things from us but for us. We are on an amazing treasure hunt, exploring the vast caverns of secrets and mysteries with Holy Spirit as our guide. Verse ten says "God has revealed them to us." We have full access to the wisdom and insight of God. These verses are stating that some mysteries will never be totally unraveled to the natural man, but through Holy Spirit and our access to God we can come into the realm of discovery. What an amazing privilege it is to sojourn into the unknown.

#Prayer

Thank You, Lord, that we are free and redeemed. Thank You that we live in Your love and acceptance. Let the power of every lie be dislodged from our minds and broken. I ask that the power of Your love, God, invade and overwhelm our hearts right now. I command every limiting accusation to be broken.

Lord, I thank You that You are a very good Father. Lord, I pray freedom for us now, in Jesus's name.

#Prophecy

God is writing great exploits upon the hearts of His people. He is releasing dreams and pictures of destiny to fuel faith and unlock potential. Open the eyes of your inner man and begin to see what He is declaring over you. Some are not able to embrace the exploits because they are trapped in the stinging memories of past disappointments.

I hear the Father saying, "My healing balm is available for these. They have not understood why it did not work. They have not been able to escape the pain and the bitter waters but I have fresh waters of redemption to release over them. I am calling My Bride forth to dream with Me—to move up higher and allow Me to write My exploits upon their hearts. I have great adventures of faith and powerful glory to reveal.

"Some have been unable to embrace the exploits because they are looking through the lens of limitation. They are seeing what they can or cannot do, but there is immeasurable power available in the inner man! There is power for exploits, breakthrough, and wonder. Begin to live, move, and advance from the spirit realm. 'I have provided *full access*—nothing lacking.'

"Some are operating under the weight of condemnation and lying accusation. Have I not said that your righteousness is of Me? I have desired to paint visions of powerful exploits upon your heart, but you were unable to see them because of lying accusations. The enemy has been hurling his lies at your mind speaking of past failures and present struggles. You must boldly stand upon My promises of freedom and appropriate the wonder-working power of My Blood! Your righteousness is of Me and is appropriated by faith. His accusations must be met with My redemption so that your heart can go free!

"A free heart is: free to love, free to dream, free to soar! Free hearts take My hand and run forward with Me. Free hearts are blank canvases for My dreams of exploits."[2]

#Activation

What lies have you believed? Have you been listening to some of the lies that I have listed in this chapter, or are there other lies that the enemy has used on you? Sit down and ask the Father to reveal the lies to you. Make it a quick list. Don't overthink it or overcomplicate it; just list them. Now pray over each lie and release the power of the blood. In each area say, "I am redeemed. Thank You, Daddy, that I am Your child and I am free!" Finish your prayer with talking to Him as your Daddy. If you have struggled at all with religion, this will make you extremely uncomfortable, but it is a huge bondage breaker! Cement yourself in the truth that He is your loving Daddy and He is good!

#TruthAndFreedom #DivineExposure

CHAPTER 8

KNOW GOD'S WILL

. . . .

Confidence in the Plans of God

N THE YEARS that I have traveled ministering the gospel, there is one question that seems to pop up more frequently than any other from people I meet: "How do I know the will of God for my life?" This seems like an elementary question, yet it is perhaps the most important concern of our lives. How do we properly discern and interpret the direction that we are to go in, the people whom we are to be surrounded by, and the adventures that we are to embark on?

We must begin to answer this question with one basic premise: God wants us to know His will more than we want to know it! He is not withholding information or guidance from us. In fact, He has provided multiple platforms upon which to communicate His desires for our lives.

Much of the blockage comes from an improper understanding of the nature of God and His desire for His people. Religious spirits have enforced a false image of God as a distant being, someone who is far off, shrouded in mystery, and far too advanced for simple human beings to understand. Embracing this false thinking about the Lord makes it difficult for us to believe God for direction and receive His leading. The heart of God throughout the ages has always been to draw us, His beloved, close to Him! In fact, all throughout Scripture He communicates His willingness to be near to us in all seasons.

> I will bless the LORD who has given me counsel; my affections also instruct me in the night seasons. I have set the LORD always before me; because He is at my right hand, I will not be moved. Therefore my heart is glad, and my glory rejoices; my flesh also will rest in security.
>
> —PSALM 16:7–9

> The LORD is near to all those who call upon Him, to all who call upon Him in truth.
>
> —PSALM 145:18

> Draw near to God, and He will draw near to you. Cleanse your hands, you sinners, and purify your hearts, you double-minded.
>
> —JAMES 4:8

It is time to change our thinking, renew our minds, and break the lie that God is distant. He is right here! There is no need for us to stumble when facing major life decisions. Our loving Father has an abundance of wisdom and guidance for us. We can break the confusion and overcome the spiritual paralysis that has us stuck in neutral or, even worse, in reverse.

We must first recognize that Jesus saved us not to be powerful ministers, world changers, business tycoons, or adventurers, but sons and daughters. Our identity can unlock both passion and potential to fulfill our purpose. We live in a society, particularly in America, that defines us by what we do. I am often surprised when I meet someone new and one of the first questions that they ask is, "What do you do?" It is as though this is the most pressing and significant thought in our minds and in our culture. Instead of asking the questions, "Who am I?" or in this case, "Whose am I?" many default to asking about what I am achieving, what great accomplishments I have, and how I measure up.

Before you check out and think that I am somehow negating the power of doing great exploits, let me say that I read the Bible as a chronicle of mind-blowing, amazing, and daring adventures. I love to read about the wars and conquering nations in the Old Testament. I can vividly see Elijah calling down fire and defeating the false prophets at Mount Carmel and Elisha raising the Shunammite woman's son from the dead. I love reading about the miracles of Jesus that shook entire cities. I am both challenged and inspired by the signs and wonders in the early church. My point is that though I believe what we *do* is not the most important thing about us, I believe God can and will give us audacious dreams. When we serve the unlimited One, we are opened up to unlimited possibilities and potential.

We are called to step out of the boat and embrace the impossible. As we think on the great miracles of Jesus, we need to recognize the key to His miracle ministry; it was the depth of His relationship with the Father. Jesus understood that His greatest calling in life was to be obedient to His Father. This is the utmost calling of our lives—to know Him and be known by Him.

But I told you that you have seen Me, and yet do not believe. All whom the Father gives Me will come to Me, and he who comes to Me I will never cast out. For

> I came down from heaven, not to do My own will, but the will of Him who sent Me.
>
> —JOHN 6:36–38

Jesus was empowered to do great things because of His absolute reliance on the Father. He understood that His life's mission was to please the Father. It is nearly impossible to fully comprehend the earth-shaking results of His three short years of earthly ministry. He achieved tremendous exploits and mind-blowing results by living a life that was planted in the epicenter of the will of God. He valued and prized the approval of the Father above the approval of man. This is critical to spiritual success.

A SIMPLE PICTURE CONFIRMS THE NEXT SEASON

Several years ago I found myself on the edge of a stunning new season. I had been in a time of seeking God for the next season in my assignment. My wife, who is the greatest life partner I could ever ask for, was in agreement that a shift was coming. Many people do not understand that there are shifts in seasons and functions in our lives. Simply put, God may have us do one thing for one season and then another in the next season. As we follow Him, He is continually releasing us to higher levels of purpose. Paul chronicled this process by describing his pursuit of "the high calling" in Philippians 3:14. He was in forward motion all of his life, pursuing the highest level of relationship, obedience, and destiny.

There is progress and forward motion as we serve God. We are not just stuck in one gear. He can change the pace, and He can change the focus. Part of our surrender is our willingness to embrace change. This has never been a problem for me as I am one of those people who gets bored easily and really enjoys new adventures. My wife, Joy, values longevity and consistency, so she is just getting settled in when I am already asking God, "What's next?" This is why we make a great team.

During this particular period God made it clear to both of us that new assignments were on the horizon. He kept communicating over and over about the transition that was coming. Many times in these types of seasons we want some type of dramatic heavenly communication, but we need to be on the lookout for the simplest of words, visions, or pictures. This is exactly what happened to me one day in prayer. I was praying and all of a sudden I clearly saw a very odd picture. I have learned through the years that when I am communicating with God and I see some type of a picture, there is usually a meaning that I have to dig out. Often God is speaking but we do not recognize His voice because of the simplicity. We have to first discern His prompting and then go after the understanding.

As I was praying, I saw what looked like an opened snack wrapper. I thought to myself, "What in the world is this?" I kept praying and pondering. Sometimes pondering is a key element in hearing the voice of God. As you ponder, pray, and then ponder some more, God illuminates your mind and the pondering turns into understanding and revelation. This is what happened to me. The Lord began to speak as I kept pondering that wrapper. He told me that the time was at hand for the transition Joy and I could sense was coming and that the wrapper represented something that had expired. If you eat food that has expired, it will make you sick! The more I prayed, the more the download came bursting into my being. It was a word that propelled me forward and reassured my heart to step out.

I could have easily overlooked the word that day and missed the whole message, but thank God, I didn't. Living a surrendered life means living a seeking life. You are open to the voice of God and looking into the spirit realm on a continual basis.

DON'T BE DISTRACTED BY TOO MANY VOICES

You will never achieve the will of God while surveying every individual and heeding their voices. The multitude of opinions can easily fuel your own uncertainty. The reality is this: when God speaks, it is settled! We do not need a second opinion, even our own. There must be a divine determination to rise above the static and tune into the voice of the One who created you. Prophetic leading begins with relationship. In fact, it is the absolute bedrock of knowing the will of God. We are called to be those who live in pursuit of the Almighty! Our lives become a mystery to the world when they perceive that we are wasting our lives; in reality we are losing our own lives to find His life inside and all around us. The deeper we plunge into God, the more His vitality overwhelms us and we live in harmony with the will of God, planted under a strong flow of Holy Spirit power.

> He who finds his life will lose it, and he who loses his life for My sake will find it.
> —MATTHEW 10:39

One of the often overlooked aspects of worship is surrender. I don't know about you, but when I think about worship, I immediately envision people lifting their hands, bowing, and engaging with music about and to the Father. The reality is that these acts of worship are momentary, but surrender is enduring. Surrender is giving control of something over to another, submitting, and letting go. Surrender empowers seeking. We are called as believers to live our lives in surrender. We pray because we are surrendered. We sing, bow, kneel, dance, and shout before the Lord because we are surrendered. We study God's Word and seek His heart from a place of surrender. We strive to live lives of obedience as godly husbands, wives, parents, leaders, and servants because we have surrendered. Deep surrender creates an atmosphere of clarity. As we are surrendered and seeking we are prioritizing the voice of the Lord. His voice empowers our advance into the realm of surrendered living. We become so aware of what He is speaking that it is much easier to identify and cast down outside voices. This is a mystery that many people cannot figure out. They look at our pursuit and think we are crazy.

Why in this world would people be so radical about God? Why would they lay down their own desires and say no to things that everyone else thinks are OK? Why would they spend quality time in gatherings learning about the ways of Jesus when they could be enjoying free time? The list could go on, but you get the picture. Non-surrendered people cannot figure out surrendered people. The answer is fairly simple though—we surrender because of love. We recognize the death of a perfect man was for us. He willingly endured a horrendous beating, false judgment, and brutal execution because He loved us. Love always requires sacrifice, and Jesus made the ultimate one for you and me.

While we were yet weak, in due time Christ died for the ungodly. Rarely for a righteous man will one die. Yet perhaps for a good man some would even dare to die. But God demonstrates His own love toward us, in that while we were yet sinners, Christ died for us.
—Romans 5:6–8

We have been radically forgiven, and therefore we are radical sons and daughters who lovingly serve our Father. We recognize His great gift of grace for us and live to please Him.

Therefore I say to you, her sins, which are many, are forgiven, for she loved much. But he who is forgiven little loves little.
—Luke 7:47

In Shawn Bolz's book *Translating God* he summarizes the power of relationship and prophetic insight by stating, "Having a deep relationship with God that includes authentic friendship will definitely lead you into sharing that kind of relationship and friendship with others. Many people pursuing prophetic gifts are about as close with God as they are their yearbook friends, but they still insist on trying to *use* prophecy on others. Then they get discouraged about the lack of relational depth developed through the experience. It's because prophetic ministry is about your being a gateway to God's thoughts, emotions, and heart for others *through connection to him.*" [1]

The foundation of prophetic ministry to others is your personal relationship with God. Your relationship with Him is also the foundation for rightly hearing, seeing, and discerning the will of God. That is the bedrock, the absolute basis, of everything. Jesus was ministering powerfully in the healing and delivering power of God. There was such glory flowing through Him that entire regions were shaken. This would be the pinnacle of success in the minds of most preachers. In the midst of this move, Jesus suddenly disappears. What could have been so important that He would leave the outpouring? What was so pressing that He would just vanish?

> In the morning, rising up a great while before sunrise, He went out and departed to a solitary place. And there He prayed. Simon and those who were with Him followed Him, and when they found Him, they said to Him, "Everyone is searching for You."
>
> —MARK 1:35–37

Jesus left the masses for an audience of One. He was more fascinated by the Father than by all the miracles. Prayer was His compass, and it was in the presence of God that His true north was discovered. A strong relationship with the Father is the foundation for exploits. We cannot rise higher without first going deeper.

KEYS TO KNOWING GOD'S WILL

Understanding God's will for your life is possible. Here are some practical ways to know what it is.

The will of God is revealed in the Word of God.

There is so much power, life, and guidance in the written Word of God. When you feel stuck and can't figure out what to do next, you need to pray and then open your Bible. Ask God to speak to you. It is amazing how He will just pour out revelation from His Word. The Bible needs to be your personal plumb line. You should judge all leadings, all experiences, and all directions from the Bible. God will never ask you to do anything that goes against His Word.

I remember a number of years ago I was counseling a minister who was going through great marriage trouble. I was never as shocked as I was the day that minister told me God had clearly spoken and he was to divorce his spouse and marry another. He went on to say that God had already shown him his next wife. My heart was so grieved at the level of deception I was hearing. I told him that this was a false word, and of course he was angry. God's voice will never speak in opposition to His Word.

> I will worship toward Your holy temple, and praise
> Your name for Your lovingkindness and for Your truth;
> for You have exalted Your word above all Your name.
> —PSALM 138:2

The will of God is confirmed by prophetic utterance.

We are to place value on prophetic insight and revelation, and it may help us discern God's will. In fact, when the Lord speaks to us, there is a release of tremendous power. We should record, write, and track every word from God to us.

> Remember the former things of old, for I am God, and
> there is no other; I am God, and there is no one like
> Me, declaring the end from the beginning, and from
> ancient times the things that are not yet done, saying,
> "My counsel shall stand, and I will do all My good
> pleasure."
> —ISAIAH 46:9–10

God's counsel stands outside time. He knows the end from the beginning. When He speaks to us, He is already declaring the end of the matter. This is one of the reasons why solid prophetic ministry is so powerful. When we receive accurate prophetic words about our lives, we are armed for battle, equipped for victory, and enlightened for what is ahead. This is not only true of prophetic words that have been declared to us by another person, but also of things that are spoken to us in private.

The will of God is communicated multiple times in multiple ways.

Pay attention to the chain of events. Anytime God wants you to know something or do something, He will speak to you multiple times or ways. If it is a particularly important assignment, He will really get the message across to you. When you get something out of left field that you have never heard before and there is no confirmation, you need to put on the brakes and pray. The apostle Paul once received a single encounter in the night that shifted his whole ministry (Acts 16:9), so I am not saying that you always will have two or three confirmations, but generally you will. I have found that every time I have made a major life decision, there were several ways and occasions when God communicated with me.

> This is the third time I am coming to you. "In the mouth of two or three witnesses shall every word be established."
> —2 CORINTHIANS 13:1

This is yet another reason why monitoring prophetic leadings is a tremendous tool. Many times we call it "prophetic history." Through it we can examine how we arrived at a particular assignment, decision, or endeavor. We have a track record of the various ways that God has spoken to us concerning a particular area, and we can put all of those pieces together to form a clear picture. Taking a big picture approach to these matters forms a very safe methodology by which to properly discern the will of God.

The will of God is a journey of stewardship.

This is one of the areas where people miss it big time. They think the will of God is some big dramatic assignment that will suddenly propel them forward. They fail to place value on the small daily tasks that actually make up the big picture. The reality is that there are no small assignments in the kingdom. Every task that God gives to us is important:

> He who is faithful in what is least is faithful also in much. And he who is dishonest in the least is dishonest also in much.
>
> —LUKE 16:10

This passage teaches us the importance of stewardship. The clear concept here is that God rewards those who steward their assignments well. We are all given different tasks, responsibilities, and talents. Yet we each have one thing in common: the same amount of seconds in a minute, minutes in an hour, hours in a day, days in a week, and weeks in a year. We often fail to realize the vital gift of time. There are people in eternity right now who wish they had more time on Earth. Each moment that passes is one that we cannot get back. We must seize the moment and rise to the occasion, executing our assignments with faithfulness and zeal.

Some seasons of life and assignments are much more difficult than others. The mom with several small children has many more limitations on her time than the mom whose children are away at college. The CEO working ten to twelve hours a day has many more demands on his time than the part-time employee. Each of us can live our best and give our best. We can be faithful and have a right heart in each thing God has asked us to do. We can also strive to be more effective in managing our time. I often hear people say, "I would love to write a book, but I just don't have time." You may not have the time, but you may be able to make time. You get up earlier, stay up later, sacrifice unnecessary things, and push through.

Don't buy the lie that all of a sudden you are going to be promoted into the will of God and then you will instantly do things well. That is a completely unrealistic thought. You must start improving and preparing now. Realize that the big assignments start with small things and little steps. In simple terms, God is not going to make you an overnight millionaire if you cannot balance your checkbook now. He is not going to send you to stadiums in other nations if you cannot minister to the people He has placed in your life now. The will of God is all around you! Your family assignment is the will of God for you in this season. The job that you are in and the people there who need ministry are the will of God for you right now. The little things that you can put your hand to right now are the will of God for you in this moment. Your commitment and faithfulness in the little will cause explosive promotion. Do not listen to the lies of the enemy that the will of God is far away in some distant place. God may have an assignment for you in an exotic location, but you must start now with what He has placed in front of you.

The will of God is reflected in a heart set after God.

This is something that many people do not understand. When we get born again, our spirit man is remade in the very image of God. What does this mean? This means that my human spirit likes what God likes and hates what God hates. It is my flesh and the enemy's temptation that causes me to get outside God's plan. As I walk with the Lord and allow my spirit to be the dominant force in my life, I should become a living reflection of the glory of God. God will give me the desires of my heart, but He also causes my heart to become established in His desires. I have an inner compass that is leading me. As my heart begins to reflect the heart of God, I can begin to use my peace level, promptings, and desires as a road map to the will of God.

Passion and devotion are two essential ingredients in the life of a believer. Sometimes we have to fight for time to spend with God reading His Word, praying, and worshipping, but it is imperative that we take on that fight. Our hearts were made to burn for Him. There is something that happens deep down inside us when we spend quality time with our Father. We tap into wisdom, revelation, mysteries, peace, and divine guidance.

> It is of the LORD's mercies that we are not consumed; His compassions do not fail. They are new every morning; great is Your faithfulness. "The LORD is my portion," says my soul, "therefore I will hope in Him." The LORD is good to those who wait for Him, to the soul who seeks Him.
> —LAMENTATIONS 3:22–25

The will of God is the inheritance of believers.

As a child of God, you were born for the will of God, and the will of God was created for you! God has perfect purpose, perfect timing, and perfect placement for you. Trusting in this reality fuels your faith and defeats fear.

#Prayer

Father, I pray for ordained pathways, kingdom assignments, and Your ultimate best for our lives. I believe we are led by Holy Spirit and obedient to His leading. Let us recognize Your voice, God, and follow Your promptings. Let us live in, move in, and walk in the will of God, free from fear or confusion, in Jesus's name, amen!

#Prophecy

Dive deeply, dive fully, dive completely. In times past you swam in the shallows of your call, experiencing momentary exhilaration as you enjoyed a portion of your full mantle. Then fear, man-pleasing, and religious pressures or lack of revelation would pull you back into the lower measure. This is the time to dive *deep* off the high dive into the high call. It's time to enjoy the full portion.

Your portion is connected to your identity. I am bringing forth revelation of who you are in Me. It creates a fearless and reckless realm of obedience that dares to jump into the deep end with no backup plan! It's the hour to dive in and not back off. It's the hour to get free from the fear of man and man's opinion. It's the hour to enjoy the full portion and take delight in Me.

I have generational exploits laid aside for those who will dive deep! For those who will dive in fully to the ultimate call on their life, there is a great treasure of great exploits and generation-shaking glory!

#Activation

What clues have you already received about the will of God for your life? What desires has He placed in your heart? Have you had prophetic words confirming those things? Get out a sheet of paper or your electronic device and make a list of at least three godly desires and three things you feel God may have spoken to you about your future. Review the list and ask God for further instructions. In the days ahead ponder those things and let Him add wisdom.

#SonsNotSlaves #Exploits #FirstThingsFirst

CHAPTER 9

DISCERN GOD'S TIMING

· · · · · · · · · · · · · · · · ·

Grace for the Wait

A s I reflect on a time when I seemed to be in a holding pattern, it seems foreign to me. I was in what I call an extended period of waiting. I was very aware of specific prophetic promises over my life, but they were not coming to pass in the time frame I expected. It was a period in which I had to really fight feelings of frustration and discouragement because my heart was longing for the fulfillment of what I was receiving from the Father.

These types of delays can be a real challenge to faith. I can vividly remember that season: I was in a church where a minister was teaching on faith, and he began to challenge people to wake up earlier and seek God at the beginning of the day. This was not a new message to me! I heard this same teaching repeatedly and always clung to the fact that I was much more of a night owl than an early morning person. Yet on this particular occasion it was as if someone took his words and branded them upon the tablet of my heart. I knew that the Lord was drawing me to rise early and seek His face. My heart was ignited with passion for the presence of God.

There is something that is so special about launching the day in the presence of God. Even Scripture discusses it:

> Give ear to my words, O LORD; consider my meditation. Listen to the voice of my cry, my King and my God, for to You will I pray. O LORD, in the morning You will hear my voice; in the morning I will direct my prayer to You, and I will watch expectantly.
> —PSALM 5:1–3

The truth of beginning the day with God became a reality in my life and shifted my habits. I became hungry to begin my days in the presence of God. I started asking the Father for grace for morning seeking. This is a truth that I have learned: when God is urging your heart to move in a certain direction, you can come before Him and ask for supernatural assistance. He not only provides the desire, but He will also get involved in the process.

I found myself suddenly waking up at all hours of the morning. I would begin to seek His face and supernatural revelation would burst across my mind as my spirit man communed with God. It was like a series of downloads. I seemed to be in a season of seeking and finding. I was living out 1 Chronicles 16:11: "Seek the LORD and His strength; seek His face continually." It was in this season of time that God began to give me an entire series of promises for my future. I could see where He wanted to take me and how I was going to get there. Each prayer encounter became richer as the Father unfolded His insight and heavenly perspective to me.

There was just one problem—I was still living in the present and my current situation did not look like my prophetic potential. After time passed, I grew weary. I examined all the powerful things the Lord had said to me but could not yet see them coming to fruition in my life. Eventually I got so frustrated that I would tell the Lord, "Please don't speak to me about my future right now!" No matter how much I pleaded, it did not stop the downloads from coming. God ignored my requests to stop the flow of information. As you become activated to see, hear, and know, you will continue to receive heavenly communication from God that is out ahead of time.

One of the challenges for prophetic people is having the patience to keep believing for what you have already seen. You are living in the space between now and the future. Your spirit sees what is coming, but you must remain faithful with what is. You are born to navigate the present while seeing the future. God had to teach me to patiently wait for the promise.

The day came when all the prophetic pictures I received during that period of time came to pass, and it was well worth the wait. While I was standing and believing for what I was seeing, it seemed so difficult, but the reality is that it was the grace of God working in me and for me to prepare me for what was to come. God will not launch you into something until you are ready for it.

You can step out in your own flesh and try to launch forth, but you will only stumble in the dark. The waiting process is necessary; something happens in the waiting. Your level of deep trust and dependency expands. Many times it is in the waiting that you discover your own flaws and weaknesses. In the waiting, there is refining. In the waiting, aligning takes place as you are properly positioned for your destiny. The waiting is not a bad period of time. It is actually a set and appointed time that holds an abundance of goodness. God invites you to discover His heart and His faithfulness in the waiting. As I waited upon the Lord, He revealed His rich and abundant goodness to me. I became so satisfied in Him that I was no longer pushing to make the promise happen.

> Wait on the LORD; be strong, and may your heart be stout; wait on the LORD.
>
> —PSALM 27:14

THE PERFECT TIME

This is one of the things that happens in extended periods of waiting. The arm of the flesh is broken so that the wells of the Spirit can be released. Those things that are birthed by human zeal without the leading, timing, and instruction of God do not carry life-giving kingdom power. There are so many believers who are simply doing things out of frustration and giving birth to projects, adventures, and journeys that are totally separated from the will of God. "And those who are in the flesh cannot please God" (Rom. 8:8). When these things do not produce enduring fruit, bitterness and frustration attempt to take root.

The enemy absolutely loves to sow seeds of frustration. Frustration unlocks a toxic atmosphere that produces horrendous fruit. When we become frustrated, we say things we would not normally say. Our mouths are powerful instruments of prophetic declaration, so the enemy is set on getting the wrong meditation in our hearts so that the wrong words come out of our mouths. He wants to do this to create evil plans in our lives. What we say matters! If the enemy can pull us out of the timing and plan of God, then he can get us in the arena of the flesh and conquer us. That is his ultimate goal.

A surrendered life is one that trusts both the leading of the Father and the timing of the Father. Part of our walk with God is trusting Him with the seasons of our life. Each season contains the potential for destiny and beauty. One of the best descriptions of seasons is found in the Old Testament Book of Ecclesiastes:

> He has made everything beautiful in its appropriate time. He has also put obscurity in their hearts so that no one comes to know the work that God has done from the beginning to the end.
> —ECCLESIASTES 3:11

When we receive a prophetic promise, we are getting a glimpse into the mind and heart of God. The revelation of prophetic destiny in our own lives is vital to our spiritual success and potential. Many people run from meeting to meeting, gathering up prophetic words and promises, yet they lack the maturity to know how to properly steward those words.

One imperative element of prophetic destiny is the realization that every promise holds time-sensitive information. Attached to each declaration is a set time of fulfillment. Prophetic promises carry a *kairos*. What is *kairos*? It is a Greek word for *time*. *Kairos* means "the right or opportune moment, the supreme moment." *Kairos* is an "opportune or seasonable time, the right time, a limited period of time."[1] When a *kairos* comes into our lives, it is time to move! It is a limited period of fulfillment. In a *kairos* there is a pregnancy of purpose that is just waiting for us to rise to the moment. It is the set time of destiny being released. *Kairos* times are pregnant with potential and ripe with breakthrough. Timing holds great significance in our individual journey and prophetic progress.

The other Greek word used for the English word *time* in the Bible is *chronos*. This word, *chronos,* deals with passing of time in chronological order.[2] *Kairos* is a set time of fulfillment and promise. *Chronos* is the unfolding and measuring of time. Every second that we are breathing, there is a *chronos* unfolding as time passes. It is entirely different than the *kairos,* which is a supreme moment of destiny being fulfilled.

The Greek word *kairos* is used several times in the New Testament. Here is one instance:

> After John was put in prison, Jesus came to Galilee preaching the gospel of the kingdom of God, saying, "The time is fulfilled, and the kingdom of God is at hand. Repent and believe the gospel."
> —MARK 1:14–15

Jesus was preaching the fulfillment of many prophetic promises. The moment of fullness had come and it was a set time for people to rise into the realization of the promise. The lion and the Lamb had come wrapped in flesh. The very living Word of God was walking and breathing amongst men, but this set time had to be recognized, received, and acted upon.

RECOGNIZE THE MOMENT!

That is the thing about a *kairos*—it is the seemingly sudden and swift eruption of destiny. *Kairos* moments require discernment and action. In a single moment a promise is fulfilled if properly acted on. *Kairos* moments do not just happen; they are the result of prophetic preparation, prayer, and obedience. I remember a *kairos* moment I had once; I was in prayer one day in my house, just spending time in the secret place, when all of a sudden I was completely swept up in deep intercession. It was so strong that I was overwhelmed by the groanings that came deep from within my spirit man. I began to see a blood red banner waving over a particular continent in the world. I was lifted in the Spirit to pray and stand in the gap for that territory. I prayed for quite a while under the strong mantle of intercession, and then it broke and I had deep peace.

Sometime later I received an invitation to speak in a church in the region I had been interceding for. Immediately I knew that I was supposed to go, so I accepted the invitation. I was going to speak for the largest church in that nation. When I arrived, there were thousands gathered, and I could feel the presence of God like electricity pulsating through the atmosphere.

There was a moment of recognition when I realized that this was part of what the Lord had me praying out. It was a *kairos*! It was not just another moment, not just the *chronos* passing of time. No, this was something far beyond that. It was a significant moment that had been well orchestrated by the master planner of the entire universe. I bowed my head before the Lord and felt Him mantling me for that moment. I preached with an unusual confidence and urgency, moving in the full potential of the moment. God's miracles erupted and unusual realms of power were unlocked.

The realization and acceptance of a *kairos* releases divine power and ability. Unfortunately you can miss a *kairos* by not having a discerning spirit. The reality is that there are set times that contain life-changing power and must be fully maximized. These moments are not the time for a spirit of fear or timidity. Fear will cause you to miss the opportunity that exists for divine breakthrough.

There are set times of refreshing and outpouring:

> Therefore repent and be converted, that your sins may be wiped away, that times of refreshing may come from the presence of the Lord.
>
> —ACTS 3:19

These times of refreshing and outpouring are the result of prayer and pursuit. Divine obedience can unlock miracle moments filled with breakthrough. Churches, ministries, revival hubs, and apostolic centers often receive prophetic pictures of what is to come. They labor in prayer, fasting and believing for the words to come to pass. The Lord then brings them to the doorway of a mighty outpouring. Though they are standing at the door, they must have the boldness and spiritual vision to open the door and walk into the promise.

The Lord spoke to me one time and told me that a lot of ministries miss the moment of visitation. I asked Him why that was, and He said it was because they simply fail to see the significance. There are times when the beginning of a move of God feels like a gathering that is slightly elevated. It can be easy to overlook and just think it is another good service. Each outpouring has a moment of ignition. That is the *kairos* time. It must be discerned and acted upon accordingly.

PROPHESY YOUR SEASON

It is the same with a personal outpouring. In our walks with God, there are times of spiritual dryness and times when we are not experiencing the sensation of the flow as we once experienced. The enemy works so hard during these seasons to plunder our hope and disappoint our hearts. His goal is to get us to just give up on the beautiful promises of our Father.

> Hope deferred makes the heart sick, but when the desire comes, it is a tree of life.
>
> —PROVERBS 13:12

These seasons are like emotional and spiritual droughts. When we are experiencing a dry climate, the answer is outpouring! We must have personal refreshing. I have found in my own life that times of refreshing usually begin with hunger. The Lord sends hunger as an invitation to pursuit. It is the hungry who are seeking, and it is the hungry who will find God. The Father has set many times of refreshing on His calendar for you. He has ordained particular seasons to pour His goodness and strength out in a significant way in your life. These moments demand your attention. They must *not* be overlooked because they need to be seized and fulfilled.

Any time that there is a change coming to our lives, there will be an announcement of that change. This is one of the dimensions of the prophetic spirit. God uses prophetic people to announce shifting times and seasons. As you develop a strong personal prayer life, you will be shown the shift in the season long before it comes.

God reveals these things to you to build your faith for

what is to come. Faith is the result of what is spoken. When you hear the voice of God and believe His voice, you are established in believing. It is the believing that creates an avenue for the breakthrough of heaven to travel into your life.

Times and seasons are framed with prophetic declaration:

> Do not remember the former things nor consider the things of old. See, I will do a new thing, now it shall spring forth; shall you not be aware of it? I will even make a way in the wilderness, and rivers in the desert. The beast of the field shall honor Me, the jackals and the owls, because I give waters in the wilderness, and rivers in the desert, to give drink to My people, My chosen ones. This people I have formed for Myself; they shall declare My praise.
>
> —ISAIAH 43:18–21

Before God took His people into their next season, He announced it to them. Prophetic declarations are instructive. If you tune your ear to what the Lord is saying to you in private times of prayer and corporate gatherings, you will often find that you are receiving similar messages that are sent to prepare you for what is coming next.

Prophetic words are alive with power. Everything that is created in the spirit realm is created by words. Words are containers that are filled with either death and unbelief or life and faith. When a prophetic declaration is released, the words contain the substance of heaven and minister life to the hearer. You must open up your spiritual ears to hear what the Father is clearly saying to you.

So many people miss their *kairos* time because they fail to effectively hear the instructions that come before the moment arrives. There are people who sink deep into a pit of defeat and discouragement simply because they did not have ears to hear the voice of God that was preparing them for transition.

You can be in the right place at the wrong time and completely miss the move of God in your life. This is why hearing and knowing are so vital. Each season holds a unique promise and challenge. When the Lord speaks about what is to come, He is equipping us to discern the doorway and move through it when it arrives.

Prophetic words are instructive. When God speaks, His mind is revealed. I have found through the years that the illumination of His mind often contains revelation. In other words, the same voice that tells me what to do will also reveal how to do it. Many people become overwhelmed by the promises of God. When He shows up and begins to reveal His plan for them, they feel unable to step into it. Some think that they are not smart enough. Others feel as though they lack the talent. Some people just believe they are not good enough for the blessing that is being revealed. The bottom line is that God thinks much bigger than we do: "For My thoughts are not your thoughts, nor are your ways My ways, says the LORD. For as the heavens are higher than the earth, so are My ways higher than your ways, and My thoughts than your thoughts" (Isa. 55:8–9). He has provided all that we need to live out His phenomenal plans for us. Many people are missing an epic life because they are not hearing and obeying the voice of God.

God has no limited dreams! He never thinks small or sees impossibility. No! God dreams, thinks, speaks, and lives *big*. When He comes on the scene and releases His supernatural power, impossible things begin to happen—miracles break forth, wonders manifest, healing flows like a river, and challenges fall over like dominoes.

> For God speaks once, yes twice, yet man does not perceive it. In a dream, in a vision of the night, when deep sleep falls upon men, in slumber on their beds, then He opens the ears of men, and seals their instruction.
> —JOB 33:14–16

When God's voice is heard, His wisdom is revealed. In this passage it boldly declares that even when man misses it, God keeps speaking. He is eager in His persistent communication with us. There are times when I meet people who tell me they just cannot seem to discern the will of God. I ask them what they think the problem is, and they tell me that God is not talking to them. I know that even though it seems that way, chances are that God is indeed communicating. They are just failing to hear it. Many times we box God in and think He must speak to us in a distinct way. The reality is that He can inform us of changing times and seasons in our lives in many different ways.

When His voice is discerned, His wisdom is revealed. Once we have recognized His talking to us about the coming season shift, we need to actively press in for instruction. This is where people easily miss it. They allow themselves to get frustrated about what seems like a delay, but it is, in fact, a process of preparation. God is not going to take you into the promise without first preparing you.

Waiting must lead to seeking. There are lessons to be learned in the wilderness. There is a degree of intimacy that is revealed in the waiting and in the period of isolation.

When we are alone with God we learn how to rely fully on Him.

It wasn't until David faced Goliath that people got a glimpse of the greatness that was dwelling in him. It took a huge obstacle to reveal the power of the anointing of God on the life of David.

> David said to Saul, "Your servant was a shepherd for my father's flock, and the lion came and the bear, and took a lamb out of the flock. And I went out after him, and struck him, and delivered it out of his mouth. And when he arose against me, I took hold of his beard, struck him, and killed him. Your servant slew both the lion and the bear. And this uncircumcised Philistine will be as one of them, because he has reviled the armies of the living God." David said, "The LORD who delivered me out of the paw of the lion and out of the paw of the bear, He will deliver me out of the hand of this Philistine."
>
> —1 SAMUEL 17:34–37

Notice what David told King Saul in the run-up to the battle with the giant. He talked about his time in the field. In a time of waiting, he squared off against things that prepared him for the promotion. This is what is accomplished in the season of waiting. There is preparation, wisdom, and character development, and weaknesses are exposed.

Far too often people receive promotions that match their level of gifting but not their character. This will create havoc every time. Character is ultimately what keeps us. Character is typically forged in the fire, not born in the times of soaring upon the winds of promotion. Often it is formed in the midst of hardship, adversity, and delay. This is what the enemy wants to abort in our lives—the absolutely critical process of formation and development for the vast destiny that God is bringing us into.

The Lord frames times and seasons with prophetic declaration.

> Afterwards the Spirit took me up and brought me in a vision by the Spirit of God into Chaldea to those of the captivity. So the vision that I had seen went up from me. Then I spoke to those of the captivity all the things that the LORD had shown me.
> —EZEKIEL 11:24–25

As you see here, God releases words of wisdom, instruction, warning, and preparation. It is imperative that we live *tuned in*. We must navigate life's journey with our spiritual antenna up, rightly discerning the leading and open to the promptings. This is a critical component of supernatural living. Miracles, breakthroughs, and radical elevations typically begin with a heavenly communication of some type. We are called to be living, breathing, prophetic expressions.

We are to continually manifest the kingdom. We are links between what is seen and what is unseen. We bring the kingdom of God into full fruition in the earthly realm. We subdue, conquer, overwhelm, and overtake by revelation and dominion. We are not people who merely *believe in* the kingdom; we are those who *carry out* the kingdom.

God gives prophetic declarations to His people. He fuels the progress and transition with divine insight and decree. As we seek His face, He fills our mouths with His decrees. He releases prayer assignments to us. This is part of the prophetic process, allowing God to guide our pursuit. He teaches us how to pray. He fills our mouths with prophetic prayers. So many people go into their place of prayer with a regimented mentality and format. I have had life-changing breakthroughs from continually standing and speaking the same thing to the mountain over and over without wavering. There is a realm of decree where you keep doing what God says. There is also a realm of prophetic praying where you birth the plans of God and give voice to the word of the Lord. In that realm you come before the Lord totally open, in deep pursuit, releasing the travail and groan of God, leaning deeply on Him. He sets the tone, the pace, and the agenda. This is part of prophetic birthing. Prophetic prayer gives way to prophetic decree. As you align your heart and mouth with what heaven is uttering, you frame the next season with words full of power and life that were born of the spirit realm. The word of the Lord is literally endued with the power to shift and move things!

GETTING GOD'S PERSPECTIVE

God grants an aerial view to His people. When they seek Him, they are lifted into the heavenly realm. They are broken loose from the captivity of limited insight, limited believing, and limited revelation. The prophetic spirit causes a person to soar on the winds of God! It releases people into new dimensions. In these times God will release prayer strategies, revealing what to pray and how to pray. He provides language and insight to secure the victory. He tasks prophetic people with prayer assignments. Many are called to live and walk in a higher level of surrender. There are miracles waiting to be birthed by those who engage the realm of prophetic prayer. The Lord appoints people to go to places on assignment. The Lord grants access into the lives of others with an assignment.

In the place of prophetic birthing, the Father gives keys of intercession. He releases key words, key revelations, and key decrees. He literally tells us what prophetic pronouncements to make to swing wide the gates of influence and authority. There are nations to be influenced and governed from the place of prayer. There are cities to be won, but they must first be brought into subjection to the kingdom of God in prayer. There are generations to be birthed in revival. Prayer is an invitation to govern.

> The key of the house of David I will lay on his shoulder. Then he shall open, and no one shall shut. And he shall shut, and no one shall open.
> —Isaiah 22:22

Most people have a false concept of prayer. They see prayer as a quiet and timid exercise. Many people even get bored in prayer. I know that there is a time to reflect, meditate, and ponder, but there is also a time to weep, prophesy, groan, and battle! We need to take our armor into the prayer closet. Too many of us have abandoned the call to war, instead embracing the seduction of apathetic teaching and believing. We have been lulled to sleep when we need to be alert and on assignment. I hear an ear-piercing alarm sound rallying the troops to man their battle stations! It is time to activate the realms of governing prayer.

Words of knowledge can become open doorways into the lives of people. I have experienced this time and time again in my travels. I will never forget many years ago when God sent me to another nation on assignment. This assignment was birthed in a time of prayer, and I diligently sought the Lord and carried the burden for that territory for a number of years. When the appointed time came, I went to that nation and faced fierce opposition. A demon appeared to me to release extreme intimidation and threats. The enemy was trying to abort my destiny in that land. Many times the measure of opposition that you face in a spiritual assignment is a confirmation of the weight upon that exploit. One night I was ministering and asked God to give me a word to open up the region. He told me that there was a deaf and mute man whom He wanted to heal. We began to look for the man and eventually found him. Jesus miraculously healed him in front of everyone! That broke open a well of miracles that is still flowing over a decade later. One word from heaven can tap a deep flow of God's power.

During that same journey the Lord granted me access to a key political leader in the nation. He became a great help to me and what I was called to do in that land. The Lord spoke to me and others who were on that team about the man's heart and dreams. We prophesied what the Lord had revealed to us and that word of the Lord granted us access into his life. Words from heaven become gateways into the hearts and lives of people. There are realms of the prophetic that must be tapped to reach a generation. There are people who will never believe even the most convincing presentation of the gospel, but a shockingly accurate word of knowledge can get the job done. I feel a massive tug from the heart of the Father for this generation to daringly plunge into the prophetic realm and release the word of the Lord over people.

I have learned that every time God invites me into a new assignment, such as those discussed above, there is also a time in which the word is destined to be fulfilled. This is a vital point of understanding for supernatural living. You may receive a word, dream, or vision that is so rich and so full of life that you just want to jump into it immediately. This is how I function. When I hear from God, I want to jump first and ask questions later. I have learned the hard way that hearing and seeing are the beginning of the process. Those prophetic pictures provide a bridge into the next season, but there is a sense of divine timing in the whole matter. I must wait upon the Lord to release me into it.

SEASONS OF LIFE

As we journey with God, it is imperative to understand that there are life seasons. I remember one time when a friend shared his frustration with me because he was feeling completely overwhelmed. He had small children, a traveling ministry, and lots of obligations at home. He was feeling totally maxed out, depleted, and under attack. I immediately remembered the season in my life when our son was a toddler and we were traveling all over preaching the gospel. It was a demanding and challenging season, yet in many ways it was so much fun. There was an intimacy and delicate nature in that season that was not present in other seasons. I can look back now and see just how special that time was, but if you asked me then, I would have probably voiced a lot of frustrations.

The reality is that each season of our lives holds promise, potential, purpose, and grace. I told my minister friend that he needed to realize that much of what he was feeling had to do with the season he was in. He was feeling the tug of a young wife who did not enjoy being alone with toddlers while her husband traveled the nations. He was feeling the tug of his children's hearts, looking for affirmation and attention from their daddy. He was feeling the excitement and acceleration of doors opening, and he was wrestling with the weight of the call of God upon his life to impact and influence nations. Each of these elements was triggering a range of emotions, and each was important. The key is to properly understand the season that you are in and to tap the potential and the promise by aligning your heart with the word of the Lord. There is a grace to achieve the mandate of the season. Grace is something that you receive and walk in; you don't earn it. There is seasonal grace for you. I told my friend that there was grace and wisdom for him during that season. I told him that he might have to say no to some ministry things and yes to some family things. He and his wife might have to discuss expectations and honestly evaluate what they could and could not do during that period of time. In all of that there was grace. There is a huge deposit of God's ability to do what we cannot do in the natural.

A lot of people contaminate their season with negative words. If you continually declare out of your mouth, "This is awful," "I am overwhelmed," or "I cannot do this," then you are partnering with a spirit of discouragement that is sent to take you out and rob you of the grace of that season. Different seasons have different rhythms, different mandates, different demands, and different promises. There is heavenly help and angelic assistance in each season. The first key is to recognize the season, and then tap the help. How do you do that? You prophesy. Replace the negative proclamation with the word of the Lord. Boldly say, "The Lord is my helper!" Activate heavenly help with your confession.

So we may boldly say: "The Lord is my helper; I will not fear. What can man do to me?"

—HEBREWS 13:6

Transitional seasons

An exciting and challenging time is a transitional season. As I mentioned, these times are typically proceeded by a prophetic encounter. The Lord will begin to stir your heart with a sense of the shift. For people who do not like change, this can be a very scary time. This is also a time of fresh calibration. The Lord is putting you in sync with another dimension of your purpose. I call seasons of transition a birthing time, and in it you carry both the burden and excitement of the next season.

During a time of transition it is vital to stay plugged into what God is saying. Just as in a natural birth there is pain, these times can be painful. Regardless, you must not get off the birthing table! I have seen the Lord transition people in the midst of a whirlwind. In what looked like a shaking, they were suddenly planted in even deeper purpose. They could have easily given up had they not had a prophetic spirit. This is why times of personal worship, prayer, and devotion are critical. It is also helpful to have solid spiritual leaders in your life to speak into your life and help you navigate the transition.

A transition means saying good-bye to one season, assignment, or role. It means there is an exit in your life. This can be difficult on your emotions. You must keep your emotions in check and walk in the Spirit during this time! Do not allow emotional upheaval to dictate your actions or set your spiritual thermostat. Let the word of the Lord guide you. As you enter into the next assignment, there is a new level of understanding, expectations, and goals. You must adjust to the next level. You may have to broaden your thinking, shake off some old paradigms, and learn some new concepts. Next-level living always requires next-level thinking, believing, and dreaming. Learning is your friend in transitional seasons. God is changing the rhythm. This can feel very uncomfortable. It is important to tap the grace and divine ability. You have never been this way before, but God has ordained your steps.

Career/work seasons

Though we are spirit beings, we live in a natural world filled with natural responsibilities. Sometimes we are tasked with frustrating job responsibilities. We are working with various personalities and asked to do things that may not be exciting for us. I can remember when the Lord sent me to Bible college. I was excited about developing the call of God on my life and plunging deep into my studies.

But even though I had a spiritual mandate, my bills didn't stop coming. I had to work and pay the bills. I was in a classroom during the day getting rocked by Holy Spirit and receiving life-changing impartations, and then at night I was working various jobs that seemed to have no meaning or purpose. Talk about frustrating.

While I recognize that there are supernatural realms of provision, prosperity, and supply, I also understand that we must put our hands to something. Even Scripture says this:

> For when we were with you, we commanded you that if any will not work, neither shall he eat.
>
> —2 THESSALONIANS 3:10

I have seen believers get sidelined during a season of hard work. They knew that what they were currently doing was not their long-term destiny, and that is where I was when I was in Bible college. The reality is that God honors diligence. Those little side jobs that seemed to have no purpose were catapulting me forward in my destiny. They were channels of provision to fuel my training. I would not be where I am today had I not rolled my sleeves up and gotten to work. Once I realized that, I began to tap into a deeper level of peace and God opened doors of ministry on the job. People would find me and share their struggles with me, and I would minister to them. My destiny found me, and it didn't matter what my surroundings were. Destiny is bigger than a temporary job or assignment. Don't be sidelined! You may be in a season of working that does not line up with your call, but God is faithful! Tap into His grace and forge ahead.

Building seasons

I had a season in my ministry when God radically shifted my assignment. I went from one level of demand to a much higher level in a short amount of time. I found myself having entire months without any significant downtime. This came on the other side of a storm that felt like it was going to take my wife and me out, but God was bigger! Everything in our ministry was tested, but God's goodness prevailed. When we came out on the other side, there was a major promotion and shift in our function. I remember one day in the midst of this season, when I was away from home to minister, I really felt tired in my flesh. I texted my wife and she quickly sent me an encouragement, reminding me that we were in a building season.

A building season requires you to plow forth. You may be

building for your financial future and juggling lots of irons. It is normal to feel overwhelmed at times, but you need to keep things in perspective. This is part of the process of advance. You are sacrificing today for a brighter tomorrow. Let's look to the Book of Proverbs for some wisdom on this subject:

> Go to the ant, you sluggard! Consider her ways and be wise. Which, having no guide, overseer, or ruler, provides her bread in the summer, and gathers her food in the harvest. How long will you sleep, O sluggard? When will you arise out of your sleep? Yet a little sleep, a little slumber, a little folding of the hands to sleep— so will your poverty come upon you like a stalker, and your need as an armed man.
>
> —PROVERBS 6:6–11

In a building season, short-term sacrifices are made for long-term rewards. Ministries are built over time and with labor. Businesses are built over time and with diligence and sacrifice. Families are built with love, investment, and sacrifice. If God has given you a vision of something greater, you must be willing to give things up in order get there. That is what investment is. You sacrifice now because you are looking at the long-term picture.

We are living in a *now* generation that wants it all and demands it quickly. The reality is that building something to last is a process. In a building season, the enemy will play on your emotions in an attempt to release weariness. This is his attempt to abort the harvest. Recognize what he is doing and remind yourself that you are building. The Lord is releasing building grace for you. The seeds that you sow today will bring forth harvest tomorrow. Stay focused, stay plugged in, stay faithful, and keep building!

Life and family seasons

> Grandchildren are the crown of old men, and the glory
> of children are their fathers.
> —PROVERBS 17:6

Different seasons in life and family will produce various rewards and struggles. I vividly remember when my wife and I first got married. There was such an excitement to build a life together. We felt as though we could conquer the world as long as we had each other. There was a tangible newness that created great excitement in our relationship. We had the bliss of a newly married couple.

As our family moved into the next season, there was a maturing in our relationship that brought even more comfort. There had to be investment and intentional attention paid to create strong foundations, but our love grew and our partnership deepened. Today we can literally finish one another's sentences. We each know how the other thinks, and there is a vast well of life experiences that we can draw from. Both seasons have been wonderful, yet they are completely different. We are able to do things today that we could not do when we first got married because of the financial growth in our lives. Our schedule is different, our options are greater, and our family is much wiser.

Seasons produce growth. When you get through one season and obey the Lord, strength and personal growth results. Each decade of your life has its own promise, potential, and challenges. If you have children, there will be different demands in each stage. You must evolve and move with the seasons of your life. Don't allow regret or missed opportunity to stagnate you! There is mercy and forgiveness for your shortcomings, and there is new life and fresh vision for the new chapter.

In addition to different seasons in family, our lives also have seasons. I firmly believe that the first third of our lives is spent discovering who we are, what we were born to do, and how to navigate the path. We can accomplish earth-changing things in our first thirty years, but there is a wisdom and stability that comes in the next thirty. At that time, we become "comfortable in our own skin." This is the gift of age and time. We can now live in our lane and be thankful for the journey. It is in this second phase that we settle into our calling and begin to soar in the true identity that we have spent years cultivating and discovering.

The final chapter of our lives should be spent pouring into our successors. While I believe this should be a lifelong goal, it intensifies and becomes the primary focus of our final chapter. We should be fully aware of who we are, what we carry, and how we can pour into others.

In every season of destiny, prophetic promise, and life, look for three things:

- The grace (divine ability) for each season. Grace produces confidence and rest. Let God captain the ship, and believe that He has prepared you.

- The word of the Lord (prophetic wisdom) for each season. Each chapter requires wisdom. Seek God for wisdom to properly travel the road ahead.

- The *kairos* (time of fulfillment) for each season. Discern the time of movement, advance, and opportunity. Your *kairos* demands recognition and response. See the door and walk into the promise. Get moving! You walk by faith, so get up and pursue the promise. Faith is not inactive; it is alive. You must respond to what heaven is revealing.

#Prayer

I pray that we are in tune with the timing of God in our lives. Thank You, Lord, for an Issachar anointing upon us to know the times and seasons. I speak powerful grace in our current season and an abundance of Your absolute peace. I pray that we see and move in Your *kairos* moments, free from fear and full of faith, in Jesus's name!

#Prophecy

The Father has opened doors into new dimensions and kingdom pathways for you. He has been preparing you for the next level and the journey of faith ahead.

I hear the Lord saying: "See the doorway and enter in. See My promise and step out. See My leading and advance. Step away from the heaviness and discouragement and enter into the promise I have for you. It is the appointed time for you to enter in. Do not stand outside the gates any longer, but come in! Come into my place of intimacy and provision. Come into the fields of harvest. Come into the leading of My voice. Come into the revelation of My spirit. Enter into that which I have prepared for you. Even in the times of testing, I have been with you. You have been refined and aligned. This is the time for you to move in what I have revealed to you with the confidence of sons and daughters. Possess the promises and be delivered of fear!"

#Activation

Sit down with a blank sheet of paper or an electronic device and ask these questions:

- What season am I currently in? (Identifying this will answer valuable questions.)
- What is the next season, or what sense of transition do I have?
- What is the potential and promise of my current season?
- Have I been cursing this season with negative declaration? (If your answer here is yes, then take a moment to repent and cleanse yourself from the false narrative the enemy has planted.)
- What grace do I need in this season? Begin to call the grace forth. Begin to boldly declare, "The Lord is my helper!"

After you have answered these, pray over your season and stay tuned in for any and all directions for the next season.

#Kairos #PregnantWithPotential

CHAPTER 10

ACT ON GOD'S DIRECTION

· · · · · · · · · · · · · · · ·

Faith Sees the Promise

HEAVENLY REVELATION FUELS earthly exploits! It is imperative that we recognize that the role of insight and revelation is to provide faith and strategy. When God illuminates something to our human spirit, there is a release of faith. God's voice produces the substance of faith into our lives. The first barrier that we break is the lie that we cannot or do not hear from God. In previous chapters, we have clearly seen that God does speak to us, He is currently speaking to us, and our born-again human spirits look like our Daddy!

The second barrier that must be broken is the confusion that arises from not being well educated on the various methodologies of spiritual communication. We have also covered that and understand that God speaks in a variety of ways. It is imperative that we discern His voice, keep track of what He has revealed, and then spend quality time seeking Him for further instruction.

ACTING IN FAITH

The instruction of the Lord will typically become a catalyst for movement. Faith is alive; therefore, faith acts:

> So faith by itself, if it has no works, is dead.
> —JAMES 2:17

Where there is no activity, there is no life. God's voice is a spark to release divine motion.

If there is no partnership with the word of the Lord, there will be no breakthrough or results. Too many people miss the miracle because they fail to recognize their role.

In Kenneth E. Hagin's article "Faith Brings Results" he writes, "It may not be manifested on the outside yet, but we know it's ours because we received it in our spirit. Many times I've known on the inside I had received a certain thing that hadn't shown up yet. But I kept my faith in God's Word, and it wasn't long before it showed up. Some things may take time, but when you believe you receive when you pray, and you're willing to stand your ground, believing you received, you won't wait long!"[1]

To move in miraculous power, you must recognize the word of the Lord and partner with it in spite of time. Faith is not moved by the passing of time. Faith stakes its claim on the promise of God and absolutely refuses to move off the word of the Lord. The enemy loves to lie and accuse. He sends all kinds of disruptive messages to your human mind. He will tell you that you missed it, that you are crazy, that God has let you down, and that your faith does not work. The Bible properly identifies the devil as an evil accuser:

> Then I heard a loud voice in heaven, saying: "Now the salvation and the power and the kingdom of our God and the authority of His Christ have come, for the accuser of our brothers, who accused them before our God day and night, has been cast down."
>
> —REVELATION 12:10

Anyone who has ever stepped beyond the limitations of the natural realm and acted upon faith has dealt with the devil's accusation. If he is not speaking, lying, and trying to persuade you to give up on your promise, then something is amiss because that is his constant obsession. He desires to break up the divine family and union of God and man.

I can vividly remember one time when my faith was greatly tested, and I failed the test. Most of the time preachers tell victory stories, but I want to give you insight into the temptation that we all face as human beings. I was preaching in a meeting, and I heard the voice of the Lord just as clearly as I have ever heard His voice. He told me to pray for a man in a wheelchair.

I got so excited about the miracle that I believed God was going to perform! This had become a common occurrence for me—God speaks, I obey, and miracles happen. That is how it works. So I prayed and acted on what I had heard and seen, but nothing happened. I had also experienced those types of situations as well. There are many variables that can accelerate or hinder a miracle. As you gain experience in the realm of the supernatural, you learn these keys.

I prayed several times, seemingly to no avail. I was looking for the instant miracle. Many times in my meetings there are tremendous healing miracles. I always teach people to grab their miracle by faith. Sometimes there is an instant miracle, and sometimes it is a progressive healing, but it really doesn't matter how it manifests. The end result is the same: victory. That night I was deeply discouraged and fell into doubt because nothing happened. I left the meeting feeling defeated. I knew God had spoken to me, and therefore I expected something powerful to happen.

Jesus was about to teach me a great lesson about the realm of the supernatural. About six weeks later, as I was sitting in my office, someone came by to visit with me. This person asked me if I remembered ministering to a person in a wheelchair six weeks earlier. Of course, I did! That individual did not get up that night, and I left troubled by the lack of power. The person in my office told me that the man in the wheelchair felt power go into his body when we prayed for him that night, and each day since he received another level of healing. I was told he was now up and out of that chair and walking!

God had performed His word! What was my error? I was moved by the passing of time. Faith does not look at how long something takes; it simply rests in the power of the promise. To experience instant miracles, there are times you have to push and keep praying. It may take diligence and a firm refusal to quit in order to crack open the realm of instant miracles and breakthroughs. Your faith invokes the dynamic workings of heaven. I have had many experiences in which I fought to get the word of the Lord to prevail over the circumstances. This is the principle of pursuit. What you pursue and believe will manifest all around you. You must believe and pursue the right things to receive from the heavenly realm. Sometimes we must rest in the act of faith, knowing that there has been a spiritual deposit. It makes no difference when the natural result comes forth because we are not looking through the eyes of the natural, but seeing by the eyes of faith. In faith, it is done—not *being done*, not *going to get done*, but *done*!

THE MINISTRIES OF JESUS

Early in my ministry I was called upon to go to hospitals and minister to people who were hardened to and even offended by the concept of divine healing. I learned quickly that this was a very ineffective strategy. Jesus did not hunt down doubting, unbelieving people and try to cram the healing ministry down their throat. No! He walked in glory and power, and the sick found Him, desiring to be healed. As they moved by faith, miracles flowed like a river. Many times a person is not healed and does not receive a breakthrough because he does not believe in that particular ministry of Jesus.

Jesus has different ministries for the world. His strongest and most common ministry is the ministry of salvation. He nailed every sin and bondage to the cross, shedding His blood and providing full access to all the glory of heaven.

> For God did not send His Son into the world to condemn the world, but that the world through Him might be saved.
> —JOHN 3:17

Jesus also endured a vicious beating to obtain our healing. Jesus has a healing ministry that is available to the entire world, but many reject that ministry and slam shut that particular door to the supernatural. They have been seduced by religious spirits. When the early church members were gathered together in the Upper Room, they were suddenly filled with the Spirit and began to speak in tongues. The early church was launched through a fiery meeting in which men preached the gospel under such unusual power that people thought they were drunk, and thousands were saved in a single day. Many reject the ministries of the Holy Spirit because of religious deception. Jesus paid for all mental and emotional torment. Soul healing is one of the life-giving ministries of Jesus. Deliverance from demon powers was a cornerstone of Jesus's earthly ministry. He never sent out disciples without charging them to cast out demons and break the powers of darkness, yet much of the modern church has soundly rejected that ministry.

To operate in the realm of the supernatural, you must embrace the ministries of Jesus. You do not get to pick and choose which ones you like and then function accordingly. No. You become His eyes and ears on the earth, sent on assignment with the fires of heaven to shake a dying world!

Jesus's Ministry Is for Today!

One time I was ministering at a youth camp with a bunch of ministers who did not embrace deliverance ministry. It was the final session, and I wanted to preach a simple message and go home. Every time I try to do that, heaven shows up and spoils my plans. You would think that I would have learned by now that I can't get by with doing my own thing. My life is surrendered to my Father. During the worship the Lord began to deal with me and I felt electricity flowing through my body. I began to pray and prophesy over the young people. God's glory filled the room.

I was drawn to a young lady to minister to her. When I came to her, demons started crying out in a man's voice.

It wasn't pretty, but then again neither was the ministry of Jesus at various points. This is one of the real issues we have in modern ministry. We think of the nice religious paintings we have of a tender-looking carpenter named Jesus, but this is not the real picture. Jesus was both the lion and the lamb. He was as fierce and masculine as He was kind and loving. Jesus was not some tame man who was unmoved by the powers of hell. He was a bold spiritual warrior who arose with fierce authority to combat and break demon powers.

Jesus has not changed. He is still healing and delivering people today: "Jesus Christ is the same yesterday, and today, and forever" (Heb. 13:8). When the demons began to manifest within the girl, I took authority over those demons and cast them out! It took a while to get them out of her, but they came out. Many of the pastors were bothered by what happened. They didn't like the fact that I stopped what I was doing to minister deliverance to the young lady. It wasn't pretty, but it was effective. The supernatural will be offensive to people at times, but the realm of heaven is tangible and brings lasting results. I would rather offend man and please God. The young lady shared her tragic story with me about ongoing sexual abuse. That was the root issue, and she received powerful freedom that night. It was worth the ridicule and rejection to get to the freedom.

Remember Philippians 2:7 (NKJV) says Jesus "made Himself of no reputation." You will not be greatly used of God if you value the opinion of man more highly than the opinion of God. You must be willing to lay your pride down at the foot of the cross. The supernatural ministry of Jesus may cost you friends; it may offend your doubting relatives and tick off your religious neighbors. I don't care! None of them died for you or ransomed you. Only one man paid the ultimate price for you. As for me, I am willing to be foolish for Him.

Believe me, there have been countless times that I have pleaded with the Lord to let me have a "nice ministry" that doesn't stir religious devils and offend carnal minds. That is not how He uses me. It is not the oil that He gave me. I am fearful of disobedience to my God. I want to be found faithful with what He has asked me to do.

I am so saddened by what I see gripping the modern church. I can hardly think of a preacher with a large national media ministry who is bold enough to cast out a demon in front of the nation. Many of the large churches in America are filled with people and prospering financially, but they never flow in the gifts of the Spirit. They refuse to allow the healing ministry of Jesus in the door. I see a picture of Jesus standing outside the building trying to get in. His heart is grieved because He wants to heal the sick. He wants to deliver the oppressed. He wants to demonstrate His supernatural power and reveal Himself as Lord! He wants to revive cities and awaken nations, but many leaders are too busy preaching their own messages, building their own kingdom, and using their own wisdom. God is calling His people back to supernatural ministry and kingdom exploits. The Book of Acts was not written about nice men who preached fascinating messages with trendy catch phrases. It was written by those who captured the heart of God and released the oil of revival that shook regions, raised the dead, broke demonic strongholds, and won the masses to Jesus. My cry is this: "Do it again, Lord!"

Three seeds, one big financial miracle

My ministry team and I were birthing a new media ministry and needed a large sum of money that we did not have in the natural. We knew that we had a word from God about the ministry. As I prayed and sought God about what to do, He reminded me of the principles of seed and harvest. I gathered my staff and told them that we were going to sow three sacrificial seeds into three ministries that were doing something much larger than we were doing. We were going to sow targeted seeds with a very particular harvest in mind.

We wrote the checks and laid hands on them petitioning heaven for powerful financial miracles. In obedience to the Lord, we released the seed and expected kingdom breakthrough. Then God had a precious person come to our ministry and sow a tremendous seed that answered our prayer and birthed a media ministry reaching the ends of the earth.

At the time it seemed absolutely crazy to sow big seeds when we needed the money for our new media ministry. This is the thing about a faith instruction—it will challenge your natural thinking. You will never launch into the realm of supernatural provision without getting out of the boat of normal sowing, normal living, and carnal thinking. You must be willing to step forth into the unknown.

When you partner with heavenly systems, you will receive heavenly results. Many people want the breakthrough and they desperately need the provision, but they will not let go of the seed. There is a spiritual law that a seed is the key to harvest. Everything in the realm of the spirit begins as a seed. The harvest is secured by releasing the seed. Great miracles will require unusual seeds. This is not just a financial law, but a spiritual law. If you want to arrive at the destination of harvest, you must travel the roadway of sowing.

> While the earth remains, seedtime and harvest, cold and heat, summer and winter, and day and night will not cease.
>
> —GENESIS 8:22

> Be not deceived. God is not mocked. For whatever a man sows, that will he also reap. For the one who sows to his own flesh will from the flesh reap corruption, but the one who sows to the Spirit will from the Spirit reap eternal life.
>
> —GALATIANS 6:7–8

Clearly hearing, seeing, and knowing the will of God opens a doorway into the supernatural. We are not natural people, living in a natural world, serving a limited God. We are, in fact, supernatural spirit beings dwelling in dimensions of the glory of God and created for phenomenal exploits. Healing, miracles, breakthroughs, and turnarounds should be normal in the life of a believer.

Jesus was empowered by Holy Spirit to perform phenomenal miracles. His ministry was one of power and encounter. He acted upon what He clearly heard and saw the Father do. I believe that His life was one that was in sync. He received heavenly downloads and unlocked the realm of miracles. He attributed His power to obedience. Jesus tapped the wells of power and released the flow through the act of obedience.

To move in the supernatural, you must recognize and honor the anointing of God:

> Then Jesus said to them, "Truly, truly I say to you, the Son can do nothing of Himself, but what He sees the Father do. For whatever He does, likewise the Son does."
>
> —JOHN 5:19

How God anointed Jesus of Nazareth with the Holy
Spirit and with power, who went about doing good
and healing all who were oppressed by the devil, for
God was with Him.

—ACTS 10:38

God worked powerful miracles by the hands of Paul.
So handkerchiefs or aprons he had touched were
brought to the sick, and the diseases left them, and
the evil spirits went out of them.

—ACTS 19:11–12

The tangible power of God was so strong in the cloths
Paul touched that incurable diseases were healed and
demons came out. The anointing of God is God's "super" on
your "natural." It is one thing to be called to do something,
but quite another thing to be empowered by Holy Spirit to
do it. Receiving anointing is like having a jet engine and
then suddenly adding the fuel. The anointing is caught. You
can catch anointing and impartation. These cloths released
an impartation and the anointing broke the power of sickness, depression, and demonization. Learning to recognize
and maximize the presence of God's anointing is vital for
supernatural ministry.

In order to effectively step out of the natural realm and
into the supernatural realm, we must learn that we are carriers of the anointing. We have the tangible presence of
God inside us. We can recognize the flow, tap the flow, and
release the flow.

But the anointing which you have received from Him
remains in you, and you do not need anyone to teach
you. For as the same anointing teaches you concerning

all things, and is truth, and is no lie, and just as it has taught you, remain in Him.

—1 JOHN 2:27

This scripture provides a stunning insight into a spiritual reality. All believers have a resident anointing. We are carriers of the presence and the glory. We must learn to overcome the lies of the enemy and our own natural mind to step out in faith and release what we are carrying.

This was brought into focus for me during a miraculous encounter. I was ministering in a conference where there was an unusual level of healing anointing. God was moving in rapid-fire miracles, one right after another. There was such a flow from my inward man that it was difficult for me to stand up under the weight of His glory. When I finished ministering that night, I literally plopped down in a chair and felt the burden to minister lift off me just as vividly as taking a coat off.

Right after I sat down, a man from the worship team came limping over to me. He told me that his hip had been crushed in a bad auto accident. In spite of the best efforts of the doctors, he was still severely affected by the injury. I could see this by the obvious limp. He wanted a miracle! There was just one problem: I felt no anointing. Earlier I think a statue could have been healed because the glory was so rich, but now there was seemingly nothing. I was frustrated. Why didn't he come earlier for prayer? He was caught up playing music and didn't want to abandon his post.

I sat there puzzled and questioning the Lord. Suddenly the Father spoke to me. "Are you still a believer?" He asked me. "Yes, Lord, I am!" I replied. He told me that I was to minster to the man, not from the anointing to preach or the anointing on my assignment, but with the believer's anointing that resided in my belly. This was the instruction I received. I arose and acted upon it and there was an instant miracle. The man took off running around the building as people screamed and praised God in awe and wonder.

God healed a gunshot wound.

I was preaching one night in Central America and flowing in healing. I was giving words of knowledge and people were receiving encouragement, strength, and healing. Then the Lord told me to begin to minister to all who needed healing. I called for the sick to come to the front. People began to get out of their seats and head forward from all over the building.

A young man came down with his arm wrapped in a bandage. It looked like perhaps it had been sprained. I tried to communicate with him, but because he was speaking to me in Spanish, I could not understand what he was saying. One of the pastors made a hand gesture and I realized that he had been shot in the arm. He had a gunshot wound. Whatever had happened had affected the bones and limited his mobility.

I prayed for him and the power of God hit him like lightning. He fell to the floor with great force and began to tremble. I watched as God's power moved up and down his body. It was something to behold. I never grow tired of seeing Jesus minister to His people. Suddenly, as the young man was shaking, his arm began swinging quickly back and forth. God seemed to be restoring the bones and healing the wounds. He came to me, unwrapped it, and moved it like nothing had ever been wrong with it. The Lord made his arm brand new! He was weeping and testified that he was totally unable to move his arm before this miracle.

Step into the realm of miracles available even today by developing faith for the anointing. Make a conscious effort to press for that anointing. Faith must be targeted. In Mark 11, Jesus told us to speak to mountains (verse 23). He was teaching us to use our faith to receive a specific thing. Use your faith to tap into the anointing. Start to believe for miracles in your personal life. Believe and pray for uncommon levels of anointing and the power of God.

Look and listen for revelation and illumination in your inner man. Open your spiritual eyes and ears. Seek for the operation of the nine gifts of the Spirit and be quick to recognize the promptings. When you see the invisible, you can do the impossible! Vision empowers the miraculous realm in your life.

David marched to the front lines of battle completely unafraid of Goliath, the giant in the land. What was it that empowered the crazy boldness of this young warrior? He had revelation about who his God was! His revelation empowered action. Many are sidelined by fear and wondering; they are in the bleachers watching others score spiritual touchdowns. The Lord is saying, "Get up and get on the field!" Prophetic revelation without obedience becomes unfulfilled longing that can easily lead to massive frustration and disappointment. We must act on the dreams, visions, and leading that God has given us. Notebooks filled with insight, words, and dreams will become binders of untapped potential if we do not have the bravery to act on the vision.

There is no life in lazy faith! Fear paralyzes and sidelines God-sized dreams. Faith stirs the human spirit to act!

#Prayer

Thank You, Lord, for rich anointing in our lives and the activation of the gifts of the Spirit. I declare uncommon levels of obedience as we seek You. I bind up the spirit of fear and timidity and stir up the gift of faith in our lives, in Jesus's name!

#Prophecy

I saw a picture of doors and people lodged in the doorway they were stuck at the entry point to another dimension. Then all of a sudden the oil began to flow! When they had oil, they easily slid through the door. The Lord is saying that as the oil is released, you will get through things that you were previously unable to endure. You will come into places, realms, upgrades, and experiences that were locked up to you before. The oil brings you out, and the oil brings you in! Receive the oil. Be unlocked— be empowered.

"For a wide door for effective service has opened to me, and there are many adversaries" (1 Cor. 16:9, NASB).

#Activation

Ask the Lord for a leading in an area in which you need a breakthrough. It may be financial, it may be in your family, or it may be in ministering to another. Seek Him for an instruction. What do you hear? Keep asking until something is illuminated and then *move*. Step out and do it! Don't look for an instant reaction; just wait and trust God. He is teaching you to hear, see, and then obey. The harvest is on the other side of obedience.

#WideOpenDoors #GoForIt #StepOut #LiveBold

NOTES

CHAPTER 1
CREATED TO HEAR FROM GOD

1. Bill Johnson, *Hosting the Presence: Unveiling Heaven's Agenda* (Shippensburg, PA: Destiny Image, 2012), 135.

2. *Merriam-Webster Online*, s.v. "temple," accessed May 22, 2017, www.merriam-webster.com/dictionary/temple.

3. *KJV New Testament Greek Lexicon*, s.v. "*sophia*," Bible Study Tools, accessed May 22, 2017, http://www.biblestudytools.com /lexicons/greek/kjv/sophia.html.

4. *KJV New Testament Greek Lexicon*, "*apokalupsis*," Bible Study Tools, accessed May 22, 2017, http://www.biblestudytools .com/lexicons/greek/kjv/apokalupsis.html.

CHAPTER 2
WAYS GOD SPEAKS

1. *Englishman's Concordance*, s.v. "*ro'eh*," Bible Hub, accessed May 22, 2017, http://biblehub.com/hebrew/strongs_7203.htm.

2. Jane Hamon, *Dreams and Visions: Understanding and Interpreting God's Messages to You* (Minneapolis, MN: Chosen, 2016), 23.

3. *Merriam-Webster Online*, s.v. "nightmare," accessed May 22, 2017, www.merriam-webster.com/dictionary/nightmare.

CHAPTER 3
STEWARD THE VOICE

1. John Eckhardt, *Prophetic Activation* (Lake Mary, FL: Charisma House, 2016), 4.

CHAPTER 4
RECEIVE INSIGHT FROM HOLY SPIRIT

1. *Merriam-Webster Online*, s.v. "grieve," accessed May 22, 2017, https://www.merriam-webster.com/dictionary/grieve.

2. *KJV New Testament Greek Lexicon*, s.v. *"meletao,"* Bible Study Tools, accessed May 22, 2017, http://www.biblestudytools.com/lexicons/greek/kjv/meletao.html.

3. *KJV Old Testament Hebrew Lexicon*, s.v. *"hagah,"* Bible Study Tools, accessed May 22, 2017, http://www.biblestudytools.com/lexicons/hebrew/kjv/hagah.html.

CHAPTER 5
THE POWER OF SPIRIT PRAYING

1. Glenn Arekion, "Tongues—The Ultimate Prayer Power," SidRoth.org, October 4, 2010, accessed May 22, 2017, https://sidroth.org/articles/tongues-ultimate-prayer-power/.

2. *Merriam-Webster Online*, s.v. "mystery," accessed May 22, 2017, https://www.merriam-webster.com/dictionary/mystery.

CHAPTER 6
CREATE A PERSONAL PROPHETIC ATMOSPHERE

1. *Merriam-Webster Online*, s.v. "atmosphere," accessed March 3, 2017, www.merriam-webster.com/dictionary/atmosphere.

CHAPTER 7
EXPOSE THE LIES OF THE ENEMY

1. *KJV New Testament Greek Lexicon*, s.v. *"katakrima,"* Bible Study Tools, accessed May 22, 2017, http://www.biblestudytools.com/lexicons/greek/kjv/katakrima.html.

2. Ryan LeStrange, Pastor & Founder, Impact International Ministries/Ryan LeStrange Ministries, "Ryan LeStrange: 'I Am Raising Up the Unlockers!'" Elijahlist.com, January 5, 2016, accessed May 15, 2017, http://elijahlist.com/words/display_word.html?ID=15554. For more information, e-mail info@RyanLeStrange.com or go to www.RyanLeStrange.com.

CHAPTER 8
KNOW GOD'S WILL

1. Shawn Bolz, *Translating God: Hearing God for Yourself and the World Around You* (Glendale, CA: ICreate Productions, 2015).

CHAPTER 9
DISCERN GOD'S TIMING

1. Blue Letter Bible, s.v. *"kairos,"* accessed May 22, 2017, https://www.blueletterbible.org/lang/lexicon/lexicon.cfm?t=kjv&strongs =g2540.
2. *Strong's Concordance*, s.v. *"chronos,"* Bible Hub, accessed May 22, 2017, http://biblehub.com/greek/5550.htm.

CHAPTER 10
ACT ON GOD'S DIRECTION

1. Kenneth E. Hagin, "Faith Brings Results!" Kenneth Hagin Ministries, accessed May 22, 2017, https://www.rhema.org/index .php?option=com_content&view=article&id=1026:faith brings -results&catid=46&Itemid=456.

Ryan LeStrange is an apostolic leader and prophetic voice. The apostolic call on his life has led him to build multiple ministries in various geographical locations, the foremost being Ryan LeStrange Ministries. Ryan, a modern-day Revivalist, moves strongly in the power of God as he travels the globe igniting Revival Fires. His conferences and gatherings are alive with Prophetic declaration, miracles, healings and powerful preaching.

Ryan is the founder and apostolic leader of TRIBE Network, a global network of ministries. He is co-founder of AwakeningTV.com, a media channel created to host revival inspired services, featuring ministers and messages both past and present.

Ryan has authored several books and is presently working on several more. *Overcoming Spiritual Attack* and *Releasing the Prophetic* have motivated believers to press for more of God. His book, *Revival Hubs Rising,* was co-authored with Jennifer LeClaire and written to incite the Church to believe and press for a move of God in their region.

INVITE RYAN @ ryanlestrange.com

CONNECT with Ryan:
www.periscope.tv/RyanLeStrange
twitter.com/RyanLeStrange
www.facebook.com/ryanlestrangeministries
youtube.com/user/TheRyanLeStrange

Ryan LeStrange
M I N I S T R I E S
P.O. BOX 16206 | BRISTOL. VA 24209

CONNECT WITH US!

**CHARISMA
HOUSE**

(Spiritual Growth)

 Facebook.com/CharismaHouse

@CharismaHouse

Instagram.com/CharismaHouse

(Health)

Pinterest.com/CharismaHouse

MEV

MODERN
ENGLISH
VERSION

(Bible)
www.mevbible.com

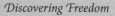